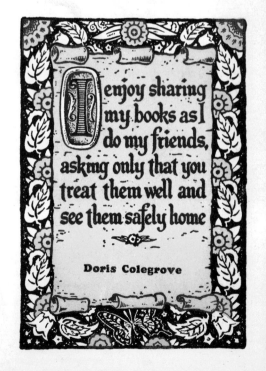

I enjoy sharing my books as I do my friends, asking only that you treat them well and see them safely home

Doris Colegrove

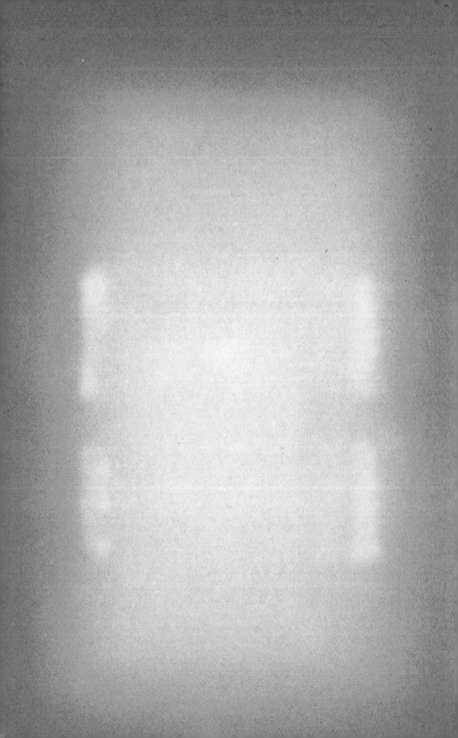

THE LIFE OF ALL LIVING

BOOKS BY BISHOP SHEEN:

God and Intelligence
Religion Without God
The Life of All Living
The Divine Romance
Old Errors and New Labels
Moods and Truths
The Way of the Cross
The Seven Last Words
The Eternal Galilean
The Philosophy of Science
The Mystical Body of Christ
Calvary and the Mass
The Moral Universe
The Cross and the Beatitudes
The Cross and the Crisis
Liberty, Equality and Fraternity
The Rainbow of Sorrow
Victory Over Vice
Whence Come Wars
The Seven Virtues
For God and Country
A Declaration of Dependence
God and War
The Divine Verdict
The Armor of God
Philosophies at War
Seven Words to the Cross
Seven Pillars of Peace
Love One Another
Freedom Under God
Communism and the Conscience of the West
The Philosophy of Religion
Peace of Soul
Lift Up Your Heart

THE LIFE OF ALL LIVING

The Philosophy of Life

BY

FULTON J. SHEEN, Ph.D., S.T.D.

Agregé en philosophie de l'Université de Louvain
Member of the Faculty of Theology, the Catholic University
of America

GARDEN CITY BOOKS

Garden City, New York

100
Sh

𝕹𝖎𝖍𝖎𝖑 𝕺𝖇𝖘𝖙𝖆𝖙: Arthur J. Scanlan, S.T.D., *Censor Librorum*

𝕴𝖒𝖕𝖗𝖎𝖒𝖆𝖙𝖚𝖗: ✠ Patrick Cardinal Hayes, *Archbishop, New York*

New York, Feast of the Epiphany, 1929

Garden City Books reprint edition 1951,
by special arrangement with Appleton-Century-Crofts, Inc.

Copyright, 1929, by The Century Company

PRINTED IN THE UNITED STATES AT
THE COUNTRY LIFE PRESS, GARDEN CITY, N.Y.

REGINAE SINE LABE ORIGINALI CONCEPTAE

PREFACE

This book is not a proof of the great truths of Christianity but a description and an analogy of these verities in terms of life. The great arcana of Divine Mysteries cannot be known by reason, but only by Revelation. Reason can however, once in possession of these truths, offer persuasions to show that they are not only not contrary to reason, or destructive of nature, but eminently suited to a scientific temper of mind and the perfection of all that is best in human nature. Such is the purpose of this book: an analogical description of Revealed Truths in terms of biology. In other words, it might be called a Supernatural Biology—a treatise on Divine Life.

In choosing this analogy we are in perfect keeping with the great patrimony of Christian tradition which is full of the analogy between the natural and supernatural life. In presenting it, we have avoided using any analogy based on a mere theory, in which case the work would be ephemeral. On the contrary, our aim has been to use throughout not hypotheses but enduring principles which are not only biological but metaphysical. In this connection it may be said that the inspiration of the whole work is the ideas contained in the 11th chapter of the fourth book of St. Thomas' *Contra Gentes.*

In these days of intellectual famine, minds are hungering for truths, as bodies, in days of food-famine, are hungering for bread. In such moments, when hunger, either intellectual or physical, gnaws at one's very being, it is not essential to demonstrate that poisons must be avoided or that food must be taken; it is enough to present the pabulum. This we have attempted to do in the following pages, and if this humble attempt achieves that purpose, by bringing even a single mind captive to the Knowledge of Life which is the Life of God, and the Love of Life which is visible in His Incarnate Son, and the Incorporation with Life which is His Mystic Body, the author will feel that the seven years spent in its preparation have been eminently worth while.

In conclusion, it is our happy duty to thank one with whom it was our pleasure to be associated on the Faculty of the Westminster Diocesan Seminary of England, Dr. E. J. Mahoney who kindly read through the manuscript and offered many valuable suggestions for making it more readable. We are also grateful to the Rev. Daniel Kennedy O. P. of the Dominican House of Studies, Washington, for the assistance which only a mind like his could give.

A final acknowledgment of indebtedness is due to the University of Louvain where this work was first begun with the suggestions of its distinguished scholar, Dr. Leon Noel, and to the Catholic University of America where it was finished, thanks to the encouragement and inspiration of its rector, the Rt. Rev. James H. Ryan.

CONTENTS

WHAT IS LIFE?

• I •

WHAT IS LIFE?

WHAT is Life? That mysterious thing which is so intimately bound up with my thoughts, my ambitions, my pleasures, and my destiny; Life—that which at times thrills me and at times saddens me; Life—that which sometimes seems the greatest of all my gifts and at others the most burdensome of all; Life—that which ushers itself in with a cry and takes its leave with a moan; Life—that which I know best and which I know least—what is it? And where is it?

The first obvious answer to this question is furnished by the senses and the very simple facts round about us, an answer which because of its very commonplaceness often escapes our notice. Life is most often associated, in the

3

popular mind, with some kind of movement or activity. If we see, for example, an animal lying motionless in a field, it gives rise to the suspicion that perhaps it is dead; it is its movement which tells us that it is alive. In like manner, when a child is seen playing with that exuberance so common to youth, we say that it is "full of life." Now this tendency, on our part, to attribute life to anything which is active is only a popular and crude explanation of what life really is. And yet most scientific descriptions are only numerical and measured statements of popular conceptions. Science does not disregard the layman's notion that life is activity; it makes it only more precise by determining the exact nature of that activity. In other words, it states that life is some kind of immanent activity. It is the addition of the word "immanent" to activity which distinguishes life from material things which are also endowed with activity, but of a totally different kind. A stove, for example, is active inas-

4

much as it diffuses its heat, and radium is active when it emits its rays, but this activity is transitive, i. e., it passes outside the thing itself. A stone is active when rolling down a mountainside, but this activity has been communicated to it from without. Living things, on the contrary, are endowed with an activity supplied from within and not from without, the effect of which remains within the thing itself as its perfection, for example, nutrition in animals and thought in man.

Modern biologists differ in their expression of immanent activity as the characteristic of life, but in substance they all insist on the preponderance of central over peripheral tendencies, and this is what is meant as immanent activity. The crystal, they urge, grows from "without" by the addition of part to part, but living particles grow from "within" by some interior principle of unity and source of movement. "Matter-in-life," such as an animal, is different from "matter-outside-life" such as carbon, and since "matter-outside-life" does not do what "matter-in-life" does, that difference must be due to something *in* the organism.

Even before the refinement of scientific instruments and before the tradition of science had enlightened us on the dominant characteristic of life, philosophers at all times in the world's history had vaguely felt the necessity of defining life as an activity produced from within. An interesting anticipation of modern biological science is to be found in the writing of Thomas Aquinas, the learned saint and saintly learned one of the thirteenth century, who after defining life as immanent activity enunciates the principle: *the greater the immanent activity, the higher the life.*[1]

This law is so universal and true that it can be verified in all the various hierarchies of the universe: viz., the plant order, the animal order, and the human order, even the angelic

[1] *Contra Gentes,* Book IV, Chap. XI.

order. Observe how it corresponds with the facts in a negative way, when we speak of the chemical order. The chemical order, which embraces the various elements such as gold, silver, iron, metal, hydrogen, oxygen, phosphorous, and the like, has no life, for the simple reason that it has no activity which emanates from within itself. A stone will not stir unless moved by some power outside itself. Michelangelo labored for months on his statue of Moses. One day the last touch was applied to it, and satisfied, he retired a few steps to gaze upon his masterpiece. There was the great legislator of the Hebrews, strong, dignified, majestic. Even Angelo himself was filled with admiration, and in a burst of enthusiasm, and in a tone of supplication, he struck the base of the statue, saying "Speak!"—but Moses did not speak. The life of Moses was only apparent. Life comes from within, and all that Michelangelo could give him came from without. Life is an internal activity, and even a

7

genius himself is incapable of communicating it to a block of marble. The statue is a beautiful one, but there is no life in stone.

But there is life in the plant for there is immanent activity. The plant has its mouth to the breast of Mother Nature, taking up from it those elements needful for its own existence. It does not grow by the mere addition of part to part like a house, but it grows from within by an expansion of its vital elements. Plant life works from the center; matter from the circumference. The life-principle within it is the source of a threefold activity which is characteristic of all plant life. First, it has the power of generation; by some dynamic power within it reproduces its kind, as each new springtime and each new harvest bear abundant witness. Secondly, it can grow, and the motive power of this increase is supplied mysteriously from within the plant itself—"Behold the lilies of the field how they *grow*." Thirdly, plant life can nourish itself. By a

8

principle and power within itself, it sends out its roots, its stalks, and its branches as so many emissaries in search of food which it does not accept by mere accretion but rather makes its own by a veritable assimilation. And if its own law of internal growth and expansion demands that a stone be pushed out of the way it will either push it aside or else turn its roots, as if conscious of its superiority over the lower kingdom in virtue of its immanent activity.

Mount up a stage higher in the scale of beings and apply the principle: the greater the immanent activity the higher the life. Is there a higher life in an animal than in a plant? The beast has a fuller life than the grass which it eats, and the bird a fuller life than the seed which it gathers from the field, and this because in animal life there is a double immanent activity added to that of plant life, viz., that of locomotion and sense perception. The animal, in addition to the generative, nutritive, and growing power which it has in common with

9

vegetable life, has an increase of immanent activity. First, it can move itself from place to place in search of richer and better pastures, or even richer and better prey. It is never a slave of its immediate environment, like the plant which must accept such sunshine and shadows, such drought and plenty as Nature gives it. More than this, the animal has the added immanence of sense perception: it can know in a sensible way the various things which it sees and hears. The dog can know its master's voice and the bird can hear the evensong of brother birds as it wings its way through the air. In other words, the animal can possess a thing within itself in a far nobler way than the plant. It can possess things within itself, not only physically by assimilation, but also mentally, namely, by sense-knowledge. And it is in virtue of its perception of sensible things, even more than by its power of self-movement, that the animal ranks higher in the scale of living beings than plants. It is the increased activity produced from within which makes the difference.

Mounting one step higher in the hierarchy of creation, we find in man a new kind of immanence added to that which he has in common with both plant and animal life, namely, the internal activity of thinking and willing. The life-principle in man is the source of a new kind of activity not hitherto found in the whole realm of creation, an activity which because of its very superiority marks him as the lord and master of creation, and that is the internal power of thinking and willing. Man can reproduce his kind, he can grow, he can nourish himself—in this he is like the plants and vegetables. Man has also the power of locomotion and the power of seeing, tasting, touching, smelling and hearing—in this he is like the animal. But nothing else is like him in his capacity for knowledge and love, for thinking and willing. In man, for the first time in the long search for perfect life, do we find a being which retains the fruit of immanent activity within itself. The term of the immanent activity of the plant is the seed, and the term of the immanent activity of the animal is its kind, and these continue their existence apart from the parent. But in man the term of his characteristic immanent activity, which is thinking and willing, remains within himself. I conceive a thought, e. g., "justice." This thought has no size, no weight, no color. I have never seen "justice" striding along a country lane or sitting down to a meal. Whence has the idea come? It has been generated by the mind just as the animal generates its kind. There is, therefore, generation in the mind just as there is generation in the life of the plant or animal, but here the generation is spiritual. There is fecundity in the mind just as there is fecundity in the lower types of life—but here the fecundity is spiritual. And because its generation and its fecundity are spiritual, the term of its generation remains in the mind; it does not fall

12

off outside it as the seed from clover or become separate as the whelp from the dog. The embryo of the animal was once a part of its parents, but in due course of nature it was born, that is, separated from the parent. But in intellectual life mental conception takes place and a thought is born of the mind, but it always remains within the mind and never separates itself from it. The intellect preserves its youth in such a way that the greatest thinkers of all times have called the intelligence the highest kind of life on this earth. This is the meaning behind the words of the Psalmist. *Intellectum da mihi et vivam,*—Life consists in knowledge. The term of its knowledge is not *this* good as with the animal, but *the Good, the True, the Beautiful.* Rising above good things, truthful things, beautiful things, it rises for that very reason, above all finite things, to a communion with the Absolute which is the Good, the True, the Beautiful.

What is true of the intellect is true of the

13

will. The power which inclines man to seek out
ends and purposes, which impels him to such
and such loves and hates, likes and dislikes, is
not something wholly outside him and therefore something wholly material. Choice comes
from within. The stone has no will; its activity
is wholly determined by a law imposed on it
from without. It must, for example, in servile
obedience to the law of gravitation, fall to the
earth when released from my hand. Just as the
material things are directed to their ends by
laws of nature so too animals are directed to
their ends by instinct. There is a hopeless
monotony in the working of animal instinct;
that is why the animal never progresses. The
bird never improves the building of its nest,
nor changes its style from the Roman to bent
twigs which express the piercing piety of
Gothic. Its activity is an imposed one, not free.
But in man there is a choice and a choice
freely determined by the soul itself. Reason
sets up one of thousands of possible targets and

14

the will chooses one of many different projec-
tiles for that target. The simple words "Thank
you" will always stand out as a refutation of
determinism, for they imply that something
which was done could possibly have been left
undone.

Not only does the choice come from within,
and not from without as it does in the law of
gravitation in the case of matter, and as it does
in this particular sensible good, a clover patch,
for example, in the case of the animal, but
the will may often seek its object in the soul
itself and find repose there. Love of duty, pursuit of truth, and the quest of intellectual ideals
are all so many immanent ends or finalities
which prove once more that man has an internal activity which far surpasses that of lower
creatures, and gives him spiritual supremacy
over them. That is why man is the master of
the universe; that is why it is his right to har-
ness the waterfall, to make the plant his food,
to imprison the bird for his song, to serve the

venison at his table. There is hierarchy of life in the universe and the life of man is higher than any other life, not because he has nutritive powers like a plant, not because he has generative powers like a beast, but because he has thinking and willing powers like God. These constitute his greatest claim to life and in losing these he becomes like to a beast.

Starting with a very elementary definition of life as activity, developing it with the findings of modern biology, and finally taking the law, the greater the immanent activity the higher the life, we have examined the various orders of creation from the chemicals on to man, finding the law verified in each of the orders. Plants possess a life and are above chemicals and minerals in virtue of the immanent activity of nutrition, growth, and reproduction; animals enjoy a higher life than plants because of their increased immanent activity of self-locomotion and sense-perception; man possesses a still higher life because of the

16

added double immanent activity of thinking and willing. And yet in none of these orders is Perfect Life to be found, though life does become more perfect as we mount up the ladder of creation. Each of these orders is sealed with imperfection because of a radical dependence upon something else, either for the conservation or the continuance of its life. Plant life, for example, could never continue without the assistance of the air, sunlight, phosphates, and the like, which it receives from without. In addition to this, for the continuance of its life it depends on another generation distinct from itself, and to this end drops its seed to the ground, where a new plant or new tree begins a distinct and separate existence. The animal, in like manner, is sealed with a double imperfection, for it depends upon external things not only for the beginning and the conservation of its life, but also for its very continuance. The animal is not an idealist, for it could never exercise its sense-perception unless there were

17

objects external to it, as it could never continue its animal life without the assistance of other creatures which serve as its nourishment. What is a more important imperfection still is the fact that the good which it seeks is never a good within itself, namely *the good,* but only *this good:* a rippling brook, new mown hay, or prey. The end of its sense-knowledge as the term of its own generative powers is something outside itself. Perfect life is not in the animal. Nor is perfect life in man though he does possess the added immanence of the faculty of knowledge and love, for the very operation of these faculties depend upon the raw materials furnished by his senses. Our mind is like a clean slate when we are born, and if we were deprived of the five senses we would never know. We must go to the visible world around about us and establish contact with it by seeing, touching, tasting, hearing, and smelling, before we can generate ideas like "Justice" and "Truth," and love these ideas as ideals.

18

While the term of the immanent activity for man, namely, the thought, does not drop from him as a seed from a plant or progeny from an animal, but remains within himself, the materials necessary for the elaboration of that thought are taken from without. There is a radical dependence in man on the external, and if Perfect Life is to be found, beyond man we must go.

But where find Perfect Life? Certainly we have no right to prejudice the case and say there is no life above man, any more than the oak has a right to say there is no life above it. On the contrary, biology insists on the principle that living things can come only from life and that spontaneous generation is impossible. But if organisms come from an egg endowed with life, and living cells from living cells, why should not all living things in this universe derive from an original Life, which must necessarily be Perfect under penalty of never accounting for even the imperfect life

19

of earth? Life can never come from below, otherwise the greater comes from the less, and that which by its nature tends to simplicity (matter) becomes that which by its nature tends to complexity (life). Peter and John walking in different directions can never meet. Reason working on the visible world does by a very simple application of the principle of causality mount up to the necessity of such a Perfect Life, free from all dependence on that which is outside it, and this Perfect Life we call God.

Like a mighty pyramid reaching from the basest of matter on to the very throne of God, there is an increasing immanence in things until we come to God where we find perfect immanent activity and therefore Perfect Life. There is no imperfection in God, neither at the beginning nor at the end of His life, for He has no beginning or end. Because He is the Alpha or the Beginning of things, He has no need of going outside Himself in search of the elements necessary for His life. Because He is the Omega or the End of things, He needs not look to another for the continuance or perfection of His life. He possesses within Himself the perfection and the fullness of Life.

But what is the nature of this immanent activity in God? To what shall we compare it? It certainly cannot be the activity of nutrition like unto animals because God has no body. It must be some spiritual activity like unto our own soul, and this is precisely what it is. Guided by revelation, we know that the internal life of God is the immanent activity of His Intellect and His Will which are identical with His very being. Because we have a spiritual substance which has an intellect and a will, we can look into ourselves for some feeble reflection of that great life of God, just as I can look at a painting of a sunset in Norway to get some idea of the reality which it represents. The study of our own soul will reveal in a feeble way the very life of God.

In the prison house of my body there is a lamp which has been lit and which will burn forever; it is my soul, the source of my life and the principle by which I live. My body will cease to live the moment this soul leaves it. Now this soul, this spirit, what does it do? It does two things: it thinks and it loves. First of all it thinks. It thinks of things beyond the confines of sense; it thinks of such spiritual things as Beauty, Truth, Love, Fortitude, Bravery, Prudence. Whence have these ideas come? Not wholly from the outside world, for no one has ever seen nor heard nor touched Justice, Beauty or Fortitude, although they may have seen a just man, a beautiful rose, or a brave soldier. These ideas, we have said, have been generated by my mind just as a plant generates a plant of its kind and an animal generates an animal of its kind. The only difference is that in the case of the mind the generation is spiritual. Now this thought, this idea or this *word* as it has been called—for even

22

before it is pronounced it is an internal word—
what is it? Is it my soul or is it something distinct from it? It is not my soul for my thoughts
come and go. I may think of art, or God or
business. One moment my thought is about
joy, another about sorrow; the thoughts which
are in my mind one minute are not in it the
next. I forget the ideas of yesterday. My ideas
and my spirit therefore are distinct one from
another. I can ask myself questions in the soli-
tude of my own mind as if I were two distinct
persons. I can be pleased with myself, angry
with myself, can enjoy my own day-dreams
and reveries, can make my life pass in review
before my mind's eye, can even be embarrassed
at my own mistakes. In a word, my internal
life is one long colloquy with myself, and yet I
am one.

Thought, however *distinct* it may be from
my soul, is not *separate* from it; when it is
present my soul sees it there; and when it is
absent it seeks for it there. I am thus one and

23

twofold at the same time. There is unity of substance and plurality of action. Though but one substance, my soul is fecund, that is, it is capable of generating thought without losing anything of itself. It multiplies without ever losing the perfection of its unity. Though I tell you my thoughts they still remain with me. I give and yet I retain. I generate and yet I lose nothing.

Now let us apply this consideration to God. And here we depend upon the revealed Word of God, for human reason left to itself could never know the inmost life of God. The reasoning which here follows is not a proof of the Trinity, but merely an analogy and an argument *ex convenientia* to show it is not contrary to reason. God is a spirit. His first act is to think. But His thought is not like ours; it is not multiple. God does not think one thought one moment and another the next moment. He does not think of you this moment and of me the next. Thoughts are not born to die and do not die to be reborn in the mind of God. All is present to Him at once. In this way His thought differs from ours, since our thoughts are distinct, one following another. In God there is only one thought; He has no need of another. That thought is infinite and equal to Himself; it reaches to the abyss of all things that are known or can be known. This thought of God, unique and absolute, the first born of the spirit of God, rests eternally in His presence as an exact representation of Himself, or as St. Paul has said, "His image, the splendor of His Glory and the figure of His substance." This thought of God is a Word just as our mind has its internal word. But God's word is One, which is one forever without being repeated— the word which St. John heard in the heavens when he began his sublime Gospel: "In the beginning was the Word and the Word was with God and the Word was God." And this thought, this *Word*, because it is generated is called a *Son*, for a son is the term of generation

25

even in the physical order. And the Active
principle of this generation is called the Father, just as the active principle of generation
in the physical order is called the Father.
When our mind conceives a thing, it has a
representation of that thing in the mind (*ver-
bum mentis*), so also, when the Father understands Himself there is the eternal subsistent
thought, the Word conceived, the object of the
Father's eternal contemplation.

> Amid the eternal silences
> God's endless Word was spoken;
> None heard but He who always spake,
> And the silence was unbroken.
> Oh marvellous! Oh worshipful!
> No song or sound is heard,
> But everywhere and every hour,
> In love, in wisdom, and in power,
> The Father speaks His dear Eternal Word!
>
> From the Father's vast tranquillity,
> In light co-equal glowing
> The kingly consubstantial Word

26

Is unutterably flowing.
Oh marvellous! Oh worshipful!
No song or sound is heard,
But everywhere and every hour,
In love, in wisdom, and in power,
The Father speaks His dear Eternal Word! [2]

This Word is called a Son because it is the perfect image and resemblance of the Father, —"the image of the invisible God," "the brightness of His glory, the figure of His substance." If an earthly father can transmit to a son all his nobility of character, how much more so can the Heavenly Father communicate to His Eternal Son all the nobility with all the Perfection and Eternity of His Being. The Son is co-eternal with the Father. The Father is not first and then thinks; the two are simultaneous. In God all is present; all is unchangeable; nothing is new, nothing is old; nothing is added, nothing is lost. And this Thought of

[2] Frederick William Faber.

27

God is distinct from God without being separated from Him just as my thought is distinct from my soul without ever being separated from it. Just as the rays of light come from the sun without ever being separated from it, as an object presented before a mirror reveals itself without destroying the original, so too in a still more sublime manner is the Son eternally generated by an Eternal Father as distinct from Him, and never separated from Him, and yet never diminishing the perfections of the Father. Thus it is that the Father contemplating His image, His Word, His Son, can say in the ecstasy of the first and real paternity: "Thou art My Son; this day have I begotten Thee." To-day—in this day of eternity, that is, in the indivisible duration of being without change. To-day—for to-day, God thinks and engenders His Son; to-day in that act which will never end as it has never begun.

Go back to the origin of the world, pile cen-

tury on century, age on age, æon on æon. "The
Word was with God." In the agelessness of
eternity—"The Word was with God." And
that Word, the Image and Splendor of the
Father, became flesh: "And the Word became
flesh and dwelt amongst us." And that Word
is no other than Jesus Christ the Second Person of the Blessed Trinity, the Word who embraces the beginning and the end of all things;
the Word who existed before Creation; the
Word who presided at Creation as the King of
the Universe; the Word made Flesh at Bethlehem; the Word made Flesh on the Cross
and the Word made Flesh dwelling, Divinity
and Humanity, in the Tabernacle—the Eucharistic Emmanuel. And the Good Friday of
twenty centuries ago did not mark the end of
Him, as it did not mark the beginning. It is
one of the moments of the Eternal Word of
God. Jesus Christ has a pre-history—the only
pre-history that is really pre-history,—a pre-
history not to be studied in the slime of prim-

eval swamps but in the bosom of the Eternal Father. Pre-history is not to be studied in rocks and the strata of the earth only, but in the incarnate Word who brought pre-history to history and has dated all the records of human events ever since into two periods—the period before, and the period after His coming. If we would even deny that He existed we must date our denial so many years after His birth.

But man not only thinks. He also loves, for he has a will as well as an intellect. Love is the second act of the soul as thinking is its first. Love is a movement toward an object loved to unite it with ourself. Love is distinct from my soul for though my soul exists throughout my life I do not love the same things. It is also distinct from my thoughts for a thought is just simply a look or a vision; for example, I say, "I see," when I wish to say, "I understand." Love, on the contrary is not a look but a movement. The animal, for example, likes the green grass and moves toward it. Though

30

love is distinct from the soul and distinct from
the thought it proceeds from both. Take an
artist, for example: his soul generates an idea
—a statue of the Blessed Mother. Suppose his
soul stopped there. Would the idea ever be
put into stone? If he did not love his idea he
would never set his chisel to work. Thus the
sculptor's love for his idea comes from his
soul, yet there is but one sculptor.

Every being loves its own perfection. The
plant loves sunshine, for it is its perfection; the
bird loves its food, for it is its perfection;
the eye loves color, for color is its perfection;
in the strict sense of the term the intellect loves
truth, for truth is its perfection. But the perfection of the Father is the Son, or the perfection of the Eternal Thinker is the Eternal
Thought. The Father therefore loves the Son.
Real love can only be the fruit of subsisting
love. The noblest love has two terms: he who
loves and he who is loved. In love the two
terms are reciprocal. I love and I am loved.

31

Between me and the one I love there is a bond. It is not my love; it is not his love. It is our love—the mysterious resultant of two affections, a bond which enchains and an embrace wherein two hearts leap with but a single joy. The Father loves the Son and the Son loves the Father. Love is not only in the Father; not only in the Son; it is something between them. The Father ravished with the Son which He engenders, the Son ravished with the Father who engendered Him, contemplate one another, love one another, give themselves and unite in love, and a love so powerful and so strong and so perfect that it forms between them a living bond, for love at such a stage cannot express itself by mere words, by canticles, by passionate cries. Love at such a degree does not speak, does not cry; it expresses itself as we do in some ineffable moments—by a breath, a sigh. And that Breath of Love is not a passing one as our own, but an Eternal Spirit and that Eternal Spirit is the Holy

32

Ghost, the Third Person of the Blessed Trinity. How all this is done, I know not, but I do believe on the testimony of God revealing that the Holy Spirit has been sent by God to rule the Church: "But when He, the Spirit of Truth, is come, He will teach you all truth" (John XVI: 13)—and that the continuous unbroken succession of the Church from the day of Christ on to our own day is not due to its organization, for that is carried on by frail vessels, but due to the profusion of this Spirit over Christ's Vicar, the Pope, and all who belong to Christ's mystical body.

Three in one—Father, Son and Holy Ghost—three Persons and one God: such is the mystery of the Trinity, such is the Life of God. How can this be? There are some faint vestiges of this life in our own soul. I know and I love. What is knowing? It is the soul acting in a certain way. What is love? It is the soul acting in another way. Though I am, though I think and though I love, my soul remains substantially one; and although God thinks and loves, the thought and the love remain perfectly within Himself, never passing outside like the fruit of a tree or the progeny of an animal. There is perfect immanent activity; therefore perfect life. God is life. The Blessed Trinity is an impenetrable mystery, not contrary to reason, but above it. Should we, however, desire some reasoned analysis demonstrating that there is no contradiction between reason and revelation, then we may take the explanation current amongst Western theologians since St. Augustine. As the trunk, the leaves and the branches go to make up but one tree; as the three angles of a triangle go to make up but one triangle; as the direction, the brightness and heat of the sun go to make up but one sun; as the length, breadth and thickness of the room make up but one room; as water, ice and steam are the three manifestations of one and the same substance; as movement, limpidity and fluidity of water do not

34

make up three rivers but one; as the form, color and perfume of the rose do not make up three roses but one; as our soul, our intellect and our will do not make up three substances but one; as $1 \times 1 \times 1 = 1$ and not 3, so too, in some more mysterious way there are three Persons in one God and yet only one God.

Life must not be sought among the dead, nor must we clothe ourselves with a shroud and call ourselves living, nor cast our lot with the life of tingling flesh which the worm consumes and the hand of death leaves cold. Life is not in wine, for the life has been crushed from the grape and its life is now the Blood of the Chalice. Life is not in earthly bread, for the life has been crushed from the wheat and its life is now in the Bread of the Altar.

Seek life wherever one will, it will be found in no one but God. "Draw the bolt of nature's secrecies; study the swift importings on the wilful face of skies." Life is not there.

"Rejoice in the evening, when she lights

her glimmering tapers round the day's dead sanctities." Life is not there.

"Laugh in the morning's eyes. Triumph and sadden with all weather; weep with heaven and make its sweet tears salt" with your own. Life is not there.

"Lay your heart to beat against the red throb of the sunset heart, and share commingling heat." Life is not there.

Delay the quest for life until "mangled youth lies dead beneath the heap of years and days have crackled and gone up in smoke." Life is not there.

Go out beyond this mist of tears and running laughter, travel across the "margent of the world," trouble the "golden gateways of the stars, smite for entrance on their clanged bars"; "say to dawn, 'be sudden,' to eve, 'be soon.' Sue all swift things for swiftness; cling to the whistling mane of every wind," "Rise from this valley of death," repose not, rest

36

not in this imperfect communion of created
life with created life; be satisfied only where
"hid battlements of eternity" are reached,
where there is life which is the Infinite Communion of the Infinite with Itself, the Original Life of all Beings, the Eternal Life whence
has emanated all that lives—God, the Life of
all living. By It the angels are immortal; by
It our souls have an imperishable existence;
by It the animals move and grow; by It the
plants have their being. If It should disappear
all earthly life would fall into nothingness for
all life on this globe is borrowed. Life is not
a push from below but a gift from above;
human life is not a perfection of animal life;
it is an imperfect representation of Divine
Life. There is no spontaneous generation in
this world, either naturally or supernaturally.
Life must come from Life. When we return
to It we live, when we depart from It we die—
and that Life—The Divine LIFE—the only

Life, the Life which all seek, many without
knowing it, is the Life of God, the Life wherein
all life rests: the Father, Son and Holy Ghost
to Whom be all honor and glory forever and
ever.

They say there is a hollow, safe and still,
A point of coolness and repose
Within the centre of a flame, where life might dwell
Unharmed and unconsumed, as in a luminous shell,
Which the bright walls of fire enclose
In breachless splendour, barrier that no foes
Could pass at will.

There is a point of rest
At the great centre of the cyclone's force,
A silence at its secret source;—
A little child might slumber undistressed,
Without the ruffle of one fairy curl,
In that strange central calm amid the mighty whirl.

So in the centre of these thoughts of God,
Cyclones of power, consuming glory-fire,—
As we fall o'erawed
Upon our faces, and are lifted higher
By His great gentleness, and carried nigher

38

Than unredeemed angels, till we stand
Even in the hollow of His hand,—
Nay more! we lean upon His breast—
There, there we find a point of perfect rest
And glorious safety. [3]

[3] "The Thoughts of God," Frances Ridley Havergal.

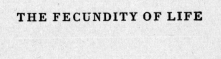

THE FECUNDITY OF LIFE

• II •

THE FECUNDITY OF LIFE

ALL life is enthusiastic. It is the very nature of life to be enthusiastic, for all life tends to diffuse and communicate itself and even to overflow its perfections in order that others may share its joy of living. The old Greeks and scholastic philosophers used to express this truth in the principle "everything that is good tends to diffuse itself." In modern times this same doctrine is more often put in biological language and expressed in these words: "All life is fecund." Both expressions, though clothed in different terminology, express the same truth, viz., that it is the nature of life to squander itself or generate other life.

There are four hierarchies of being to which this principle can be applied—the chemical,

43

the plant, the animal, and the rational. While
there is no life in the chemical order, there is
a diffusion of the goodness which it possesses.
Water diffuses itself in steam. The sun diffuses
itself in light and heat. The oxygen which is in
the air diffuses itself in the waters of the sea,
making possible the life of the fish which live
therein.

In the plant kingdom there is not only a
diffusion of matter but also of life; in other
words, there is real fecundity. The oak is good
and diffuses itself in the generation of the
acorn. The tree is good and diffuses itself in
the generation of fruits; the vine is good and
diffuses itself in the generation of the grape;
the bush is good and diffuses itself in the generation of the rose; the flower is good and diffuses itself in its perfume; the plant is good
and diffuses itself in the generation of other
plants.

The animal too is good and diffuses itself
in the generation of its kind. The sheep is good,

and the fields abound with frolicking lambs; the bird is good, and the air is filled with the sweet song of its young. Even the smallest kinds of animals we know are not foreign to this law. There is a kind of animal so small that it cannot be seen by the naked eye but only under a powerful microscope. It is the paramecium which has only one cell. It moves; it selects its food; without lungs it can respire; without stomach it digests food; without heart or blood vessels it circulates the food within its structure, and without sense organs it is sensitive and responds to stimulation. The usual method by which these animals diffuse themselves is by cell division. A new cell begins to form on the parent cell, finally separates and grows, and this in turn repeats the process; thus two or three generations may be formed within an hour. But whether one considers the life of these paramecia or that of the elephant, the principle still holds true in the animal order. Life is good and goodness dif-

45

fuses itself. Nature knows no exception to the law that life is fecund. Life generates other life.

Man has life and life is fecund. We dwell not on his physical fecundity for in this he is like to an animal—the process is the same. But we pass on to that higher kind of fecundity, namely, the generation and diffusion of thought. Whenever we think, the mind begets an idea of the thing known which is spiritual like the faculty in which it resides. This forming of ideas by the mind is a veritable generation, the product of intellectual fecundity. The idea generated does not drop outside the mind as the seed drops from the plant, or the fruit from the tree, or the progeny from the animal. The idea remains in the mind after it has been generated, distinct from the soul, and yet not separated from it, for when it is present, my soul sees it there, and when it is absent, my soul seeks it in the mind. But the mind is not only fecund in generating intellec-

46

tual life; because it is good it tends to diffuse itself. The highest kind of communication is the communication of thought, and it is the sublimity of this communication which is the measure of the greatness not only of individuals but also of civilization. All teaching is based on the possibility of such diffusion. It is thought which rules the world. "The thinker lives forever; the toiler dies in a day."

In the material order then, the diffusion is existential; in the plant order, the diffusion is vital; in the animal order, the communication is sensitive; in the human order, the diffusion is intellectual. With an increase of life there is an increase in the immateriality and *finesse* of its fecundity. Like a mighty pyramid rising to its peak, life rises with an increased stress on the spirituality of its fecundity. And yet in none of these orders do we find the source of the fecundity of life.

Where seek it? Why is life fecund? If there is imperfect fecundity in imperfect life, shall there not be perfect fecundity in perfect life? If the picture representing the rose is beautiful, shall not the rose be more beautiful? If Murillo's "Immaculate Conception" is inspiring, shall we deny inspiration to the artist? If the ray of sunlight is bright, shall not the sun be brightness? If we receive only one 2,200,000,-000th part of the light of the sun, may it not be that we receive also just a faint participation of that which is Perfect Fecundity? No one can give that which he does not possess. Shall not the giver of life have Life? Shall not the giver of goodness be Good?—not with that imperfect life which is a mélange of death, and not with that imperfect goodness which is a mélange of badness, but with that life which is nothing but Life, and that good which is nothing but Goodness? Shall not the Giver of fecundity be fecund? In the revealed words of Sacred Scripture: "He that planteth the ear shall he not hear? He that formeth the eye shall He not consider? Shall not I that make

48

others bring forth children Myself bring forth,
saith the Lord. Shall I that give generation to
others Myself be barren?" [1]

But what is the nature of this Divine Fecundity? If everything that is good diffuses itself,
what is the nature of the diffusion of Perfect
Goodness? It is twofold: internal and external. Internal diffusion is revealed to us in
the Blessed Trinity. God, it was said, is fecund.
From all eternity he engenders His Word. The
Father thinks; He thinks a Thought. That
Thought is a Word, and the Word because
generated, is called a Son. This infinite term
of the infinite Fecundity is necessarily unique,
because in the Infinity of the Son, infinite
Fecundity finds its complete adequacy. And
since love in its real meaning is the attraction
of those who communicate in life, it follows

[1] Fecundity in the natural order does not prove fecundity in
the spiritual order. But given the knowledge of the Trinity by
Revelation, the fecundity of Divine Life is not at all unreasonable. Rather it discloses the reason of all earthly fecundity. The
Creator does not diffuse Himself because creation diffuses itself,
but rather creation diffuses itself because the Creator has first
diffused Himself.

49

that there is a subsisting love between the Father and Son, and this subsisting love which is distinct from both, though not separate, is the Holy Spirit.

This diffusion of Infinite Life in the communion of the True and the Good does not exhaust the Fecundity of God. There are yet other kinds of diffusion which are free and external, and which depend upon the free choice of Almighty God. God has no need of these external manifestations. He has no need of space for His sojourn, for His life is immense. He has no need of time in which to exist, for His existence is eternal. He finds in Himself the life of Infinite Variety, the amiable society of the Three Persons in God. He is His own Temple, His own Duration, His own Existence and His own ravishing horizon. If He wishes to create, or become Incarnate, or to live a mystic Life, it is, in the words of St. Thomas Aquinas, "Not on account of usefulness but on account of goodness." From the

free impulsion of His heart, without any con-
straint or duty or the inducement of merited
love, God manifests Himself externally. He is
therefore the only perfectly Liberal Being, because He alone acts not for His own benefit,
but because of His goodness. A human being,
for example, in drawing forth another from
his generous bosom performs an act of full and
absolute sovereignty. He is father because he
has willed it, as God is a Creator and Father
and Head, because He has willed it.

But though God freely wills to reveal Himself to creatures He does it only progressively.
He does not immediately draw the veil that
hides His august majesty. He merely gives His
creatures little glimpses and reserves the full
vision for heaven. As centuries whirl around
into space, He permits us to catch a few and
furtive glances of His ineffable Greatness. And
each new revelation has made Him better
known and better loved. Have we not sometimes seen the sunlight passing through a

51

prism and noticed how it was broken up into the seven colors of the spectrum varying from deep red to deep violet? In just such a fashion as this the wonderful nature of God is broken up for our intelligence in the three-fold diffusion of Divine Life: *Creation, the Incarnation and the Church;* God shines through the prism of Creation and reveals His existence and His attributes; He shines through the prism of the Incarnation and reveals His inmost nature; He shines through the prism of the Church and reveals the Life of His Incarnate Son. If God had never chosen to reveal Himself by these progressive manifestations, we should never have been able to know Him well, just as we could never have seen the colors hidden in the white light of the sun unless they had passed through the prism.

The first act by which God revealed His riches is Creation. But why did God create the world? God created the world for the same reason we find it difficult to keep a secret—

because it is *good,* and goodness tends to diffuse itself. God could not keep the secret of His Perfections, and the telling of the secret to nothingness was Creation. God is good and He wills that others share in His perfections. Goodness sums up all the perfections of God. But all perfection, as the human mind visions it, implies some object to which that perfection can be applied. We could never say that a man was a perfect sculptor, unless he had marble on which to exercise his art. We could never say that Fra Angelico was a great painter, unless he had a canvas whereon to touch his brush. Now God is the Infinite Artist. Where find that vast and profound "object" on which He can exercise His artistry? Where find that which is as needy as Divine Goodness is bounteous? Where find that "object" which is as abysmal as His goodness, in order that abyss might cry out to abyss? God has found it. From the center of His Perfection He beheld that which is without beauty, shape, form, life or name, that "being" without being, which we call nothingness. He heard the cry of worlds that were not, and the cry of unmeasured misery calling to unbounded goodness. He found nothingness worthy of His Artistry, not in the sense that "nothingness" was a thing or an object or a raw material, but rather the absence of all being.

Eternity moved and said to Time: Begin. Omnipotence moved and said to Nothingness: Be. Light moved and said to darkness: Be light. Order spoke and said to Chaos: Rule. Out from the finger-tips of God there tumbled planets and worlds; stars were thrown in their orbits and spheres into space. The great march of worlds began, and yet with all this novelty and newness, His goodness was not increased. There were more beings after Creation than before, but no more Being; there were more good things but no more Goodness; there were more true things, but no more Truth; there were more merciful creatures but no more

Mercy. How could there be more when all creation is nothing but a reflection of the Divine Being, Goodness and Truth? Just as my own image is revealed in a mirror without ever destroying the original, so too in a far superior way is God revealed in creation without losing anything of Himself. There is no diminution of His substance in creating, any more than there is a diminution of the substance of the seal when it leaves its imprint on wax.

Just as the waters of the sea reflect the light of the moon and mirror its glamour, so too does all visible creation reveal the attributes of God. And because no creature could possibly reflect all His perfections He multiplied and diversified creatures, so that what one lacks the other might supply. Thus the totality of the universe, like a great orchestra made up of many instruments, proclaims His perfections more than any one creature, however perfect, could do. Every object which the mind can discern is a letter of the living Word of God. Some men, always children mentally, play with the alphabet blocks as so many meaningless toys, never dreaming to spell the word, until it is too late—when the universe is taken away. Others, there are, who see meaning in the blocks, and it is these who learn to read the sentence that stands first in the primer of life: God made the world.

A man places his hand on some vile clay. The clay bears the imprint and likeness of his hand. God creates—the act of creation is common to the Three Persons—and the imprint of the hand of God is left in creation. More than that, there are vestiges of the Three Persons of the Blessed Trinity, vestiges, however, which we could never discern without Revelation. Do we not commonly attribute Power to the Father? Do we not say in the Creed: "I believe in God the Father Almighty"? Do we not commonly attribute Wisdom to the Son? Does not Sacred Scripture call Him Eternal

Wisdom? Do we not commonly attribute Love to the Holy Ghost? Does not the revealed Word of God call Him the Spirit of Love?

How does one show forth Power? Is it not in doing many things? Imagine then—for we must imagine successively that which takes place in one act with God—God the Father throwing golden fires into the vast realms of space, and orbs and pairs of orbs and brother-hoods of orbs, into their flashing circuits. An infinity of things is made, some as small as the grain of sand and others as large as the mountain . . . As we gaze upon the mighty works which God has wrought, do we ever think of the Father Almighty?

How does one show forth Wisdom? Is it not in establishing laws? Imagine then God the Son at the same moment these great things were created giving them laws, establishing harmony among the unimpeded crowds of worlds, and a magnificent gentle self-confi-dence of order in which stars rush by stars,

57

and planets by planets without a hitch or halt. . . . Do we ever think of the Wisdom of the Son in our study of the laws of nature and the vision of order and harmony of creation?

How does one show forth Love? Is it not by attraction or by inclination? Imagine the Holy Spirit giving to the universe the great law of gravitation in virtue of which all things tend to the center of the earth, which is but a material-expression of the great spiritual law that man with an immortal soul naturally tends with all his energy to that great center of spiritual Gravitation—His God and Maker. . . . Do we ever think of the love of the Holy Spirit in seeing a stone fall from our hand to the earth?

But this manifestation of the riches of God is very meager. They are merely vestiges of the Trinity and not revelations and we would never know they were vestiges unless we had known the Trinity. I may see, for example, the

58

painting of the "Crucifixion" by Fra Angelico in the Convent of San Marco in Florence. I may stand enraptured before this great masterpiece, and may divine something of the nature of the artist, the depth of his inspiration, the *finesse* of his technique, and the beauty of his soul, but still I have much to learn about him which his word, his look or his very person would reveal to me. The picture would never reveal his inmost thoughts. So it is with Almighty God. The white light of His nature shining through the prism of creation breaks up into faint expressions of His Infinite Perfections. As great as creation is, and as eloquently as the heavenly spheres speak forth the wisdom of God, there is nothing in it which reveals the inner life of God. A stone, for example, resembles me inasmuch as I have existence; a plant resembles me inasmuch as I have life; an animal resembles me inasmuch as I am conscious, but there is nothing in all visible creation which resembles me in that one thing which makes

59

me a man—namely, my intellect. So it is with God. A stone reflects God, because it has existence; a plant reflects God, because it is living; an animal reflects God, because it is conscious; a man reflects God, because he has an intellect and a will, but there is nothing which reflects the inmost life of God, Divinity.

Hence some other manifestation is necessary to reveal this inner and perfect Life of God. Once more God shines through a prism, this time not through the prism of Creation, but through the prism of the Incarnation. One night there went out over the stillness of the evening breeze, out over those white chalky hills of Bethlehem, a cry, a gentle cry, the cry of a new born babe. "The Word became flesh and dwelt amongst us." Earth did not hear the cry, for the earth slept; men did not hear the cry, for they did not know that a Child could be greater than a man; the sea did not hear the cry, for the sea was filled with its own voice; kings did not hear the cry, for they did not know that a King could be born in a stable; empires did not hear the cry, for empires did not know that an Infant could hold the reins that steer suns and worlds in their courses. But shepherds and philosophers heard the cry, for only the very simple and the very learned—never the man with one book— know that the heart of a God can cry out in the cry of a Child. And they came with gifts—and adored, and so great was the majesty seated on the brow of the Child which lay before them, so great was the dignity of the babe, so powerful was the light of those eyes that shone like celestial suns, that they could not help but cry out: "Emmanuel: God is with us." God revealed Himself to men again. This time He shone through the prism of the Incarnation and brought Divine life to human life. He who is born without a mother in Heaven is born without a father on earth. He who made His mother is born of His Mother. He who made all flesh is born of flesh. "The bird that built the nest is hatched therein." Maker of the sun, under the sun; Moulder of the earth, on the earth; Ineffably Wise, a little Infant. Filling the world, lying in a manger; ruling the stars, suckling a breast; the mirth of Heaven weeps; God becomes man; Creator a creature. Rich become poor; Divinity incarnate; Majesty subjugated; Liberty captive; Eternity time; Master a servant, Truth accused; Judge judged; Justice condemned; Lord scourged; Power bound with ropes; King crowned with thorns; Salvation wounded; Life, dead. "The Eternal Word is dumb." Marvel of marvels! Union of unions! three mysterious unions in one: Divinity and humanity; Virginity and fecundity; Faith and the heart of man. And though we shall live on through eternity, eternity will not be long enough for us to understand the mystery of that "Child who was a father and of the mother who was a child."

For the first time in the history of the re-

deemed universe is the Divine Life hypostat-
ically bound up with human nature. That very
life of God that passes from Father to Son
in the eternal generation of the Trinity, now
passes into the world and assumes a human
nature like our own, graces it with the plenitude of His Divinity, and gives us that message
of hope: "I am come that you may have life
and that in abundance"—not the physical life
which dies, but the spiritual life which endureth unto life everlasting.

Men now began to hear answers to those
terrible questions which the Greeks had asked:
If God is alone, how is He happy? If He is
one, what does He think about? If He is alone,
whom does He love? The answer was the
Trinity, that inmost life of God, that fullness and fruitfulness of Knowledge and Love
which is the source of the ineffable bliss of
the society of the Three Persons in One God.
And as He who brought the secret of the Trinity walked over the earth seeking for a place

63

to lay His head, while the foxes had their holes and the birds their nests, the world began to understand how much God must love the world when He sent into it His only begotten Son. And when He told men the story of the prodigal son and taught them to pray thus: "Our Father," then they realized what a blessed privilege it was to be a brother of Jesus Christ, and a son of the Father. And finally when men heard a cry ringing out over the muffled sound of steel sinking through sinews and fibers of hands raised only to bless: "Father, forgive them for they know not what they do," they began to understand the worth of a soul. It was as if the lesson were being driven in their souls like a spear into His heart: the lesson that certainly, in the words of St. Augustine, if a "man is sufficient for a God, then God ought to be sufficient for man."

And yet, if Christ is the Eternal Son of God, true God and true man, if added to the mys-

64

tery of the Trinity there is now added the mystery of the Incarnation, how can thirty-three years of earthly sojourn exhaust its beauty or reveal its plenitude? If an eternity is not long enough to contemplate the beauty of the Son, how could thirty-three years be long enough to contemplate the beauty of the Word made flesh? That short span did little more than suggest the beauties of that Divine Life amongst us. Palestine as a space, and three and thirty years as time, cannot sound the depths of Infinite Life. Feeble minds simply had to have that brilliant Light—"I am the Light of the world"—broken up for them. The life of Christ must shine through the prism once more that it may easily enter into puny hearts. And so the white Light, *Lumen de Lumine,* shines through the prism of the Church, and Christ is revealed in it and His Sacraments.

And the Church, be it understood, is not a church in the sense that it is a sect; but it is a spouse, "the Spouse of Christ." It is not a religion of authority in the sense that it demands an irrational credulity, but a religion of the Word, for Pentecost was not the descent of a book on the heads of the Apostles, but tongues of fire. The Church is not only an institution, it is a *Life:* the continuation, the diffusion and the expansion of the Divine Life which the Incarnation brought to this earth.

The Church is Christ and Christ is the Church, and until this equation is understood, there can never be an understanding of how Christ prolongs His Incarnation beyond Galilee and His infallibility beyond the first years of the Christian era. The Incarnation is the union of the Word with an individual human nature. The continuation of the Incarnation is the union of Christ with every individual human nature in the world. The personal union in the Incarnation is the prelude to the mystical union in the Church. In becoming Incarnate the Word assumed a human body which became the instrument of His mes-

66

sages, His teachings, His miracles, and even His Redemption. Possessing a body He could suffer as man; being God His sufferings had an infinite value. But He "assumed" another body; this time not an individual, physical one, but a mystical one, a body made up of all baptized souls, and this mystic body which is the Church has as its head the historical Christ born in Bethlehem and crucified in Jerusalem. The union of the two, viz., the body, which is the baptized members and the head, the historical Christ, make up the Mystic Christ, or the Church. Just as all the citizens of this country under the headship of our President constitute the American nation, so too the union of all baptized under Christ constitutes the Mystic Christ, or what St. Augustine called the "totus Christus" or the Church. Is not this the sense of the words of Paul: "No man ever hated his own flesh: but nourisheth it, as also Christ does the Church, because we are members of His body, of His flesh, and of His bones." And did not this same fiery vessel of election, when he was yet Saul, have that lesson driven home to him the moment of his conversion. Saul hated the Christians, as few men ever hated them. Armed with letters, he set out for Damascus to bind those who were there and bring them to Jerusalem. Suddenly a light shines round about him, and he hears a voice saying, "Saul, Saul, why persecuteth thou Me?" The heat of the Eastern sun fires his lips to speak and nothingness dares ask the name of Omnipotence, "Who art thou?" and the voice answers, "I am Jesus Whom thou persecuteth." Saul is persecuting the Church, and the voice says, "I am Jesus Whom thou persecutest." Christ and the Church—are they the same? Precisely, we are other Christs as an individual fact, and the Church is the Mystic Body of Christ, as a social fact.

Herein lies the fundamental difference between the Catholic Church and all other forms of Christianity. The non-Catholic believes with the Catholic Church that Jesus Christ was God, and that after His mortal life He ascended into Heaven, but it limits religion to the individual's relation with Christ. The Catholic, on the other hand, contends that man is not only an individual, but also a member of society, hence religion is social as well as individual. It teaches the individual that Christ just as really and truly lives now in His new and mystic body, as He did during His physical life, though of course in another way. The Incarnate did not exhaust Himself in the Incarnation; that is why He may continue to live in a new way; that is why Christ told Saul that in persecuting the Church of Damascus he was persecuting Him; that explains the words of Our Lord to Peter, who, while fleeing persecution, met the Master and asked Him, "Whither goest Thou?" The answer of the Savior was, "I am going back to Rome to be recrucified."

Thus the constitution of the Church is

modeled upon the Incarnation. In Christ there was a Divine and human nature, in the Church there is a Divine and a human element. The Divine in it is Christ, the human is the body, i. e., the poor, weak human members who make it up. The Divine and the human natures in Christ enjoyed unity, thanks to the Divine Person; so too the Church is one, though made up of an infinite and a finite element. Furthermore, just as in Christ there was a visible and an invisible nature, the invisible being the Divine Nature and the visible the human nature, so too in the Church the invisible Head is Christ and the visible body is its baptized members. Even here I find the reason for the very weakness of the Church. In assuming a human nature the Word took one like unto us in all things save sin; it was subject to human weakness, to thirst at Jacob's well, and to fatigue in Galilee. The body of the Church too, though "assumed" by Christ since the Incarnation, is not free from its weakness, either

70

physically, morally or mystically, since the body is moral and mystical. The moments of its Transfiguration are few, but the moments of its fatigue more frequent. And if there be a scandal in the Church, and if another Judas blister its lips with a kiss, I can see Christ continuing His life in the Church, not only in His strength, but also in His weakness.

And now as regards the Infallibility of the Church, what is that but the Infallibility of Christ? The Church is infallible because Christ is the Church. There is no such thing as Christ merely conferring immunity from error to His Mystical Body like one might give a diploma or a deed. It is *intrinsic* to it, a condition of the very continued life of Christ, and the Holy Spirit which He sent to keep it from error even to the consummation of the world. This infallibility of Christ is exercised in the Church through visible means. I make a resolution, for example, to read a poem. The resolution is spiritual and invisible, but the act of reading

71

takes place through material and visible means, namely through my eyes and optic nerves. So too in the Church the Spirit of Christ, which is the Truth of the Church Invisible, expresses itself through visible means, i. e., through a visible head, the Vicar of Christ, the Pope. The Truth is one and the same, the expression alone is different as a thought is spiritual in my own mind but vocal in my speech. It is therefore nonsense to refuse to accept the word of the Visible Head on the grounds that it is not the word of the Invisible Head Christ; we might just as well refuse to use our hand because our Invisible will commanded it. "If two can be in one flesh," asked St. Augustine, "why cannot there be two in one voice?" This certainly is the meaning of the words of Our Lord: "He that heareth you heareth Me."

By this same reasoning I am driven to the conclusion that there can be but one Church. The Church in Sacred Scripture is called the "body of Christ." If it is a physical monstrosity for one head to have many bodies, would it not be a spiritual monstrosity for Christ to have many bodies, as many Churches teaching contrary and contradictory doctrines? The Church is also called in Scripture "the spouse of Christ," and matrimony is said to be its material symbol, for a husband is told to love his wife as Christ loves the Church. If it be physical adultery for one spouse to have many spouses, would it not be a spiritual adultery for Christ to have many "spouses" as many Churches? The very logic that made us as children doubt the reality of Santa Claus because we saw a different one in different stores, makes us also conclude as grown-ups the impossibility of many sects as the "spouse" and "body of Christ." The mind by the very necessity of its operation is driven to seek unity.

It is this notion of the Church as the body of Christ which is growing in age and wisdom and grace "unto a perfect man, unto the measure of the age of the fullness of Christ," which supplies the key to the understanding of its life of prayer and sacrifice. As my body is made up of many members, hands and feet, head and arteries, and so forth, so too is the body of Christ, the Church, made up of many members. The hand is not the foot, the bishop is not the layman; the heart is not the artery, the Vicar of Christ is not the priest, and yet all go to make up the harmony of the body. "If one member suffer anything, all the members suffer with it; or if one member glory, all the members rejoice with it." And just as in the natural order blood may be transfused from one member of society to another to save a life, so too in the spiritual order, not blood, but prayers and sacrifices and penances, may be transfused from one soul to another. If skin can be grafted from one member to another, why cannot mortifications be grafted? And this grafting, this transfusion of spiritual realities to the wounded, anemic members of the

74

Mystic Body, is especially the work of those souls who have left the world for the peace and shadow of the cloister where the saints are made. The world asks of the Carmelites and of the Poor Clares in their cells: "What good do they do?" forgetting that they are atoning and repenting for the sins of the world. Certainly if a flower is more noble when it gladdens a sick room than when it lives its life only with the other flowers of the garden, then a human being can be more noble when it serves that which is above it, namely, the Lord Who died for it, than when it serves those of its own kind. And it is this service of the Lord that gives the peace which the world cannot give.

The Church then is the continuation of the Incarnation. It is the Kingdom of Jesus Christ: "It is His Throne, His sanctuary, His tabernacle. Let us say something still more profound. It is Jesus Christ diffused and communicated."

Few have brought forth more beautifully than Father Benson this great spiritual truth that Christ is the Church:

"For I see through her eyes, the eyes of God to shine, and through her lips I hear His words. In each of her hands as she raises them to bless, I see the wounds that dripped on Calvary, and her feet upon her altar stairs are signed with the same marks as those which Magdalene kissed. As she comforts me in the confessional I hear the voice that bade the sinner go and sin no more; and as she rebukes or pierces me with blame, I shrink aside trembling with those who went out one by one, beginning with the eldest, till Jesus and the penitent were left alone. As she cries her invitation through the world I hear the same ringing claim as that which called, 'Come unto me and find rest to your souls'; as she drives those who profess to serve her from her service I see the same flame of wrath that scourged the changers of money from the temple courts.

As I watch her in the midst of her people, applauded by the mob shouting always for the rising sun, I see the palm branches about her head, and the City and Kingdom of God, it would seem, scarcely a stone's throw away, yet across the valley

76

of Kedron and the garden of Gethsemane; and as I watch her pelted with mud, spurned, spat at and disgraced, I read in her eyes the message that we should weep not for her but for ourselves and for our children, since she is immortal and we are but mortal after all. As I look on her white body, dead and drained with blood, I smell once more the odor of the ointments and the trampled grass of that garden near to the place where He was crucified, and hear the tramp of the soldiers who came to seal the stone and set the watch. And, at last, as I see her moving once more in dawn light of each new day, or in the revelation of the evening, as the sun of this or that dynasty rises and sets, I understand that He Who was dead has come forth once more with healing in His wings, to comfort those that mourn and to bind up the broken-hearted; and that His coming is not with observation, but in the depth of night as His enemies slept and His lovers woke for sorrow.

Yet even as I see this I understand that Easter is but Bethlehem once again; that the cycle runs round to its beginning and that the conflict is all to fight again; for they will not be persuaded, though One rises daily from the dead." [2]

[2] Benson, "Christ in the Church."

But if the Church is Jesus Christ diffused and communicated, how is He diffused? How communicated? He is communicated chiefly by the Holy Sacrifice of the Mass and the seven sacraments. The Mass is an act, not a prayer recited. It is the immortal sacrifice of Christ renewed on our altars. And the Sacraments, are they only myths? Oh! do we forget that our whole social life is intertwined with "sacraments" in the broad sense of the term, inasmuch as what they hold they hide, and they bring what they veil. The clasping of hands, the kiss—we do not chafe at them, or should not. A kiss may be a poor way of expressing and indeed conveying love; even by a kiss we may betray, as Judas did. Yet true lovers do not feel their kiss divides them, comes between them or caricatures their love simply because it is physical and external. It is an expression of what they feel in their hearts. Now the Sacraments are the kiss of God where He not only pours out the riches of His

78

love, but satisfies the hungers of the sense and thought as well as the soul.

The Sacraments are the communication of the life of God. And there is a parallel between the physical and the spiritual life. What elements are necessary for our physical life? Are there not five for the individual physical life and two for our social life? As individuals, first, we must be born; second, we must grow; third, we must nourish ourselves; fourth, we must heal our wounds; and fifth, drive out all traces of infirmity and disease. As social beings, first, we must have order and government; and second, we must pass on our life to posterity. These seven elements are required in the spiritual order and the seven make up the seven Sacraments. First, we must be born: that is Baptism; second, we must grow spiritually and reach the stage of Christian virility: that is Confirmation; third, we must nourish our souls on the Bread of Life: that is the Eucharist; fourth, we must bind up

79

our spiritual wounds: that is Penance; fifth, we must root out all traces of spiritual infirmities: that is Extreme Unction. But we are also social beings. We need government and a source of unity and the priesthood: that is Holy Orders. We need to continue the existence of the race: that is Matrimony.

Thus the spiritual life is a perfection of the physical life and the seven Sacraments instituted by Christ are so many channels of that Divine Life whose reservoir is Calvary.

"We approach and in spite of the darkness our hands, our head, our brow or our lips become, as it were, sensible of the contact of something more than earthly. We know not where we are, but we have been bathing in water and a voice tells us that it is blood. Or we have a mark signed upon our foreheads and it speaks of Calvary. Or we recollect a hand laid upon our heads and surely it had the print of the nails upon it and resembled Him who gave sight to the blind and raised the dead. Or we have been eating or drinking; and it was not a dream surely that One fed us from

80

His Wounded Side and renewed our nature by the heavenly meat He gave us." [3]

Beginning with a simple fact confirmed by daily observation, namely, that all life is fecund, and understanding that fact in terms of the principle: goodness is diffusive of itself, we have been led to a greater and better understanding not only of the material world, but the spiritual world as well. Very simply, the rose that diffuses itself in its perfume is feebly revealing the key which helps us to understand the three great manifestations of God's goodness—Creation, the Incarnation, and the Church. There comes out of these considerations not only the lesson of the impossibility of a conflict between science and true religion, but also the more sublime lesson of the glory of motherhood. The source of all fecundity is God: "Shall not I that make others bring forth children, Myself bring forth, saith the Lord."

[3] Cardinal Newman.

God has a Son, generated spiritually from all eternity, and to the eternal confusion of birth control propagandists who would render life sterile, let it be recalled that all fecundity is derived from God. In bringing forth children into the world parents are not like animals; they are like God. They are not productive of their image and likeness because the flower or the beast is productive; they are productive because they are imitating God in their own way, carrying on the work of Creation, and preparing bodies for the Spark of Life which He breathes into them. Controlling artificially the diffusion of human life is putting goodness in chains. The first preachers of birth control were the soldiers of Herod who sought to kill all the male children under two years of age.

In retrospect, witness that long and beautiful Procession of Life. First there is an Eternal Procession of that Life from Father to Son in the unity of the Holy Spirit. Then by a free act of God, and from out this Infinite Ocean of Life, life comes like an uncreated splendor. There is an instantaneous flash, the first visibility of the invisible God, and there lay outspread the broad world of angels, throbbing with light, and the brightness that silvered them was the reflection of Divine Life. Then there is a flame of an intolerable battle and the flash of arch-angelic spears, and Michael's war-cry summons his hosts to victory.

The Procession of Life moved on. A fiat is pronounced to nothingness, and planets and worlds drop from the finger-tips of God and tumble into space. There is a wonderful and palpitating thing moving about these worlds and lingering on the banks of Eden's four-fold river. It is the life of God in Adam and Eve. Then there is a stir among the fallen angels and paradise is overcast with shades; divine life passes out of the world and an angel with a flaming sword is stationed at the gates of the garden of paradise lest returning they should eat of the fruit of the tree of life and live forever.

The Procession of Life moved on. An angel darts out from the white throne of Light, out of the West and out of the darkness that lay over the earth. Over the plains of Esdraelon he wheeled and down to the city of Nazareth. A Virgin was there kneeling in morning prayer. She lifted her head, and an Angel from the throne of Light stood by her side. "Hail, full of grace, the Lord is with thee." These were not words. They were the Word. The Word that was come to abide with her. "And the Word became flesh and dwelt amongst us."

And the angel's wings outstretched in parting threw the shadow of a cross across the cave.

The Procession of Life moved on, and the shadow became a reality, and one day the blood of the Word made flesh dried on the cross of Calvary, and a soldier came and opened the side with a lance.

And the Procession of Life moved on—the Procession of Blood and Water; blood the price of our redemption and water the symbol of our regeneration.

And the Procession of Life moves on—back again to God:

"All that began with God, in God must end;
  All lives are garnered in His final bliss;
  All wills hereafter shall be one with His:
  When in the sea we sought, our spirits blend.
  Rays of pure light, which one frail prism may
      rend
  Into conflicting colours, meet and kiss
  With manifold attraction, yet still miss
  Contentment, while their kindred hues contend.
  Break but that three-edged glass:—inviolate
  The sundered beams resume their primal state,
  Weaving pure light in flawless harmony.
  Thus decomposed, subject to love and strife,
  God's thought, made conscious through man's
      mortal life,
  Resumes through death the eternal unity." [4]

[4] John Addington Symonds, "The Prism of Life."

THE FIRST LAW OF LIFE: EXPANSION

· III ·

THE FIRST LAW OF LIFE: EXPANSION

A STUDY of the nature of life prepares us for the understanding of its laws, for life grows and develops with an unmistakable display of order. The ordered process of life is twofold. In strict scientific terminology these processes are called the anabolic and the katabolic. In more simple terms the anabolic law of life is that life must consume food and nourish itself, the katabolic law of life is that life must not only consume but be consumed, in other words, it must surrender its lower life if it is to live in a higher life and thus escape degeneration, decay and death.[1]

Continuance of life demands a balance, or

[1] Purely katabolic activities involve release of energy and result in true excretion products, but certain new substances are sometimes formed in metabolic processes which are purely katabolic. Production of such substances is often called constructive katabolism.

89

an equilibrium between assimilation, or the processes which build up, and dissimilation, or the forces which tear down. Hence scientists say that growth means a balance in favor of assimilation, and decay means a balance in favor of dissimilation. In the mineral kingdom these two processes are found though in a different way. Metals expand when heated and contract when cooled. What expansion is to matter that anabolism is to organisms, and what contraction is to matter that katabolism is to organisms. It is the first of these laws with which we are at present concerned, namely, life must expand and nourish itself.

First of all, plant life shows itself obedient to this law, for it goes to the chemical kingdom for the food which is necessary for its existence. Its drink is the water, and its meat the phosphates and carbonates in the earth. It pumps up the water against the attraction of the earth and circulates it through its organisms. If the mineral kingdom which stands below the plant in the order of creation, were blotted out of existence, the vegetable kingdom would soon cease to exist. If the sun were annihilated; if the soil were powerless to send up its gases and its food into the roots of the plant; if the clouds were no longer able to send down their showers of rain, then flowers and plants and trees would cease to live for life can live only by communion with something else.

The animal, because its life is higher than that of the plant, is in still greater need of nourishment. It needs not only the nourishment of the mineral order—the air, the sunlight and the like—but also the nourishment of the plant life. From the very moment the animal comes into the world, until finally it lays itself down in the sleep of death, there is a quest for nourishment. The fundamental instinct of its life is to seek its food. The skylark at the moment the sun is setting, mounts into the sky, to sing a last adieu to that light

91

before it sinks into the flaming void of the west. It is but chanting its *Te Deum* in thanksgiving for the food it received during the day from the bountiful hand of Providence. The quadruped roaming in the field, the fish swimming in the ocean, the eagle soaring in the air are all in search of nourishment and daily bread, for without knowing it, they acknowledge that life is impossible without nourishment, that life grows only by life, and that the joy of living comes from a communion with another kind of life.

And as for man—need we here recall the rigorous application of that law? Because we have a body just as animals, we are under the necessity of feeding that body. It clamors for its own food just as rigorously as the body of an animal. And the food for which it clamors is more delicate, because the human body is more delicate. Our body is not content as the plant, to take its food from the ground, raw, uncooked and unseasoned. It seeks the refinement that comes with a higher creature, and in doing so acknowledges that universal law of life: that every living thing must nourish itself. Life lives by life, and the joy of living is enhanced by communion with another kind of life.

But man has a soul as well as a body. Does this spiritual part of him demand food which is above the material? Or does the soul demand a food beyond the confines of this world? Can the soul find its food in the kingdom of earth, its playthings and its tinsels? The answer of the modern world is that it can. It calls a halt to this law, that all life must nourish itself, and asserts that the soul can find a satisfying food here in this great cosmos of ours without appealing to any other or spiritual world. And what is this food which, it is said, will satisfy the soul? The world of to-day answers, it is twofold. First, science; Secondly, service of humanity. Science is said to satisfy the soul because it satisfies man's craving for truth. It gives man a knowledge of the order and harmony of the heavens, the strata of the earth, the history of races and the rise and fall of civilizations. It is the key to the great secrets of nature's chest and there is a naturalness about such knowledge, it is maintained, for it makes no appeal to that which is beyond the retort, the test tube and the microscope.

The second kind of food for the soul, according to the modern world, is the service of humanity. It gives man a chance to rejoice in the communion with his fellow-man, and it permits him to worship at the shrines his own hands have made. The popular expression of a humanitarian is: "I give to the poor and help the widow and the fatherless"; "I lead a good honest life, do good to my neighbor; I treat every man as my fellow"; "My creed is one of social service." The implication throughout all this is that man needs nothing outside of men to satisfy his soul.

But does this earth, and the men who are

94

in it, suffice to feed the soul? Are the conclusions of science nourishment and food for the soul, or do they make hungry where most they satisfy? Science cannot be a satisfying food because it cannot give us the freedom we desire. Science is built on the premise of a world determined to certain effects under certain conditions. To make a new discovery is to add another link to the network of things, and to multiply the weight of determinism which the soul seeks to escape in virtue of its spiritual nature. Furthermore, no science can answer all the enigmas of life. Some of the questions the Lord put to Job recall the insufficiency of a knowledge of natural causes: "Where wast thou when I laid the foundations of the earth? . . . Upon what are its bases grounded, or who hath laid the cornerstone thereof? Who shut up the sea with doors when it did break forth as issuing out of a womb? Where is the way where light dwelleth, and where is the place of darkness? Didst thou

95

know thou wouldst be born and dost thou
know the number of thy days? Who is the
father of rain? . . . or who begot the drops
of dew? Out of whose womb came the ice; and
the frost from heaven who hath gendered it?
Shalt thou be able to join together the shining
stars the Pleiades, or canst thou stop turning
about the Arcturus? Canst thou bring forth the
day star in its time and make the evening star
to rise upon the children of earth? Canst
thou lift up thy voice to the clouds that an
abundance of waters may cover thee? Canst
thou send lightnings and will they go and
will they return and say to thee: 'Here we
are.'?"

The religion of humanitarianism is equally
unsatisfactory in satisfying the hunger of the
soul. First of all, is it not a strange paradox
that men who most wildly disclaim against
religion are those who wish to make a religion
out of irreligious humanity? Humanity can
never be the object of religion for the very

reason that a self-centered humanity would be just as chilling as a self-centered individual. Furthermore, there is no such thing as humanity, practically speaking. There are only men; only Peters and Pauls, Marys and Anns. And it is nonsense to speak of altruism, if there be only humanity, for humanity has no "alter," no "other," toward which it can be beneficent. It is only when men call God "Father," that they can call one another "Brother," and God is not a Father unless He has a Son. Even the serpent in the garden knew that the service of humanity could never satisfy man. He tricked man, not by telling him he would be like other men, but that he would be like unto God.

Neither science nor service of humanity then can satisfy the hunger of the soul. There is nothing on this earth which can satisfy this soul hunger of man, for the very reason that it is an unearthly hunger. Every kind of life in this universe demands a nourishment

97

suited to its nature. A canary does not consume the same kind of food as a boa-constrictor because its nature is different. But man's soul is spiritual in its nature, therefore it demands a spiritual food.

An earthly love will not completely satisfy because it cannot answer the craving for perfect and lasting love; a truth of natural science will not satisfy because it is but a small fraction of the full-orbed truth the mind seeks. It is only after a long time and with much difficulty that man ever comes even to the knowledge of all natural truths. What then will that food be which will satisfy the cravings of a spiritual soul which is ever haunted by infinity? Had man been created and left in a state of pure nature, his soul would have fed on such knowledge and love of God as could be obtained from creatures. But, because of man's elevation to a supernatural state he desires and needs the spiritual beyond his natural capacities. This spiritual food given freely was a knowledge of revealed truth and a love of all that Revelation implied. In addition to that God gave a food which is not only a wonderful nourishment but a more wonderful elevation of our poor nature to a communion with the Divine.[2]

Jesus Christ is the Bread of Life; He promised He would be and He fulfilled the promise. The promise was given at Capharnaum: "The Bread that I will give you is My Flesh for the life of the world." The fulfillment took place the night before He died, when He, who was Lord of all things, had nothing to leave in His last will and testament except that which no one else can give—Himself. And that testament was given not in halting metaphors and

[2] This does not mean to assert that the need of the Eucharist for the natural man proves its necessity but only that the Eucharist once revealed and instituted does not conflict with the ordinary working of the laws of life but rather is their perfection. The necessity of the Eucharist cannot be proven apart from special revelation. Had there been no special act of Christ's love, we could not have *imagined* such a food.

99

limping figures of speech, but in cold straight forward words cut like the facets of a diamond:

This is My Body;

This is My Blood.

Between Capharnaum and the upper-room, between the promise of Bread and the giving of Bread, there was the question of those who labor after the meat which perishes: "How can this man give us His flesh to eat?" But for both those who depart, saying: "This saying is hard and who can hear it?" and for those who remain saying: "Lord, to whom shall we go?" there was no doubt that He meant what He said. And this has always been the singular title upon which the Catholic Church rests her doctrines—she believes that Jesus Christ meant what He said and not something else. When He said to His chosen priests, "Whose sins you shall forgive they are forgiven," we believe, and we have the Sacrament of Penance. When He said: "My Truth I give unto you . . . I am with you all days even unto

100

the consummation of the world," we believe and we have infallibility. When He said, "This is My Body," we believe He meant what He said, and we have the Eucharist. We do not believe He meant, "This signifies My Body," or "This signifies My Blood," for that is not what He said.

From that eventful night on, men have believed in the Eucharistic Emmanuel. Within almost two decades after the Ascension, we find Paul reminding the Corinthians, a sea and a civilization distant from the cradle of Christianity, not to eat the Bread or drink the Chalice of the Lord unworthily, for it makes one "guilty of the Body and Blood of Christ." Certainly such warning would never have been hurled against them, if the Bread and Wine were only symbols of the Body and Blood.

Years pass on. A hunted Savior must have hunted children, and He who is born under the earth must feed His children under the earth. Persecutions arise and the cave-children

101

of the King dig into the bowels of the earth like human moles; there, under roads that rocked with the tramp of Cæsar's resistless legions, under the foundations of Rome's very temples, these lovers of the Life nourished themselves on the Bread of Life. Then out from their vaults and caverns they came to gaze upon a thumb-down crowd of the Coliseum. The arena was circular: there was no outlet, no means of escape, except from above —but that was enough. They met death with a smile of joy upon their lips. Cæsar's servants scattered fresh sand to hide their blood, but they could not still their voices. They arose from the shambles of Rome's circus to reach the very chancery of God's justice, to pierce the mist of undawned ages with no uncertain challenge: "In our blood has been mingled the Blood of the Living God, dying and behold we live."

And the Church of which they had been militant members, came also from out its vaults and caverns, and it too lived, because its life was the Life of God. Lamps began to flicker and lights to jump with joy before thousands of tabernacles in a thousand lands. And no one during all this time thought of denying the Real Presence of Jesus Christ in the Eucharist. It was reserved for Berengarius in the year 1088 formally to deny it—a denial which was later retracted. It has been only since the beginning of the sixteenth century that the world has devitalized religion, made the Church a structure, and the Bread of Life only a figure and a symbol.

But in the Church—the Mystic Body of Christ—there has been an undying loyalty to the Eucharistic Presence, not only in the most humble tabernacle of a foreign mission, but also in the great jubilee demonstration of a Eucharistic Congress. It is the Eucharist that makes the difference. The center of the House of God is not a pulpit nor an organ, but Christ Himself; it is not a city, like Mecca, but a Life

—the Life of God. The Church does not merely point her finger back two thousand years and say: "Let Christ be your example." That is all the modern milk and water Christianity has to offer—just a memory of Christ who lived twenty centuries ago. No wonder it is unsatisfying to hearts that hunger for realities. If that were all Christianity meant, namely, a memory, then the memory of Christ must differ but little from the memory of Seneca or Cicero, of Washington or Lincoln. If Christ means no more to our lives than the example of His life twenty centuries ago, then it is difficult to see how He was God and how He differed from man. If He had no power to extend His life, His influence, His grace, His very Body and Blood, through time to its very end, then He is under the same limitations of every man. Life demands more than a souvenir to sustain it, and if Christ is the very Life of Christians then He must be more than a memory.

It would not be enough to tell the animal:

104

"See the way the plant lives, let that be your example." If Christ is to be our Food and our Life, it is fitting that He be with us, for it is of the very nature of Life to be localized and definite. The plant life which is the food of the animal does not dwell in some distant planet, and neither does Christ who is the Food of the Soul, dwell apart from us like an absentee landlord. He is with us, He is here, He has a dwelling. The tabernacle is now *de facto* the localization of life, and it is there and there only that the downcast eyes of sin find wealth of purging tears; only there, that the longings of hope are uplifted to look beyond the veil; only there, that the scourged heart that bleeds and bleeds afresh, at last breaks its silence in answer to the invitation: "Child, give Me thy Heart."

And what a contrast and sad spectacle is presented in the churches of our separated brethren who have denied that Christ meant what He said in saying He would give Him-

105

self to man under the appearance of bread and wine! What a tragedy it is to enter their edifices otherwise so beautiful, only to find that the soul is not there. A home is not a home unless there are dwellers; a church is not a church unless Christ is there. Entering such buildings, one almost feels he is standing alongside the tomb on Easter morn and an angel is there in white saying: "He is not here."

But the process of life, the revelation granted, demands not only the localization or the Real Presence of Life, but also communion with that Life. Communion with God is a free gift, a gift which might not have been given, but this does not alter the fact that given, it is something which eminently suits the very nature of man. Communion is not something contrary to the workings of nature, but rather the crown and glory of its orderly processes; it is a law of all living things which have not perfect life within themselves.

If the chemical could speak it would say to the plant: "Unless you eat me you shall not have life in you." If the plant could speak it would say to the animal: "Unless you eat me you shall not have life in you." If the animal and plant and the air could speak they would say to man: "Unless you eat me you shall not have life in you." With the same logic, but speaking from above and not from below, because the soul is spiritual, Jesus Christ can and did actually say to the soul: "Except you eat the Flesh of the Son of Man and drink His Blood you shall not have life in you." Having called man to a supernatural end God gave the means to that end, and among these means the one we here single out to show how it perfects nature, is the communion with Himself in the Eucharist. The law of transformation works consistently throughout the whole order of nature and supernature. The lower transforms itself into the higher. The plant transforms itself into the animal when taken into it as food, but man is transformed by grace and love into Christ when he takes Christ into his soul as food, for it is the quality of love to transform itself into the object loved.

In the Holy Sacrifice of the Mass, the bread and the wine are changed into the Body and the Blood of Christ. The word "transubstantiation" has been applied to that act; it means that the substance of the bread becomes the substance of the Body and the substance of the wine becomes the substance of the Blood, but the outward appearances, tastes, color, weight, shape—in a word, all the sensible appearances—still remain. There is a kind of transubstantiation which takes place in Holy Communion; we say a "kind of" because it is not identical in all respects. When I receive Holy Communion I receive Christ; this does not mean that my substance becomes His substance, nor that there is a fusion of the two. But it does mean that Christ comes in me to vivify me and to transform my activities so

108

that I love what He loves, I hate what He hates, I will what He wills, His interests become my interests; His affections become my affections; His desires become my desires. In this sense I can cry out with Paul: "I live, no, not I, but Christ liveth in me." And though my activities are transformed, my bodily appearance, my address and my exterior, my name and my occupation remain unchanged. The appearances still remain, but down deep in my soul a wonderful change has taken place: I have given way to Christ. "Christ liveth in me," [3] St. Augustine has expressed this thought in his prayer:

"O Truth, O Infinite Beauty, O External Love, O Superabundant Life. Thou Who changest by miracle and on thousands of our altars, the substance of bread and wine into that of Thy Body and Blood, deign to accomplish yet another change. Transform into Thyself my spirit, my heart, my

[3] The decree of the Council of Florence, Pro Armenis (Denz. 698) declares: "Huius sacramenti effectus, quem in omnia operatur digne sumentis, est *adunatio hominis ad Christum*."

imagination, my whole being. May the power of Thy oblation and the permanent serenity of Thy Love, operate that marvelous change in the obscurities of exile, till the day in which we shall be eternally consummated in the light of day without decline. Amen."

I am not surprised that He gives Himself to me as food. After all, if He furnishes food for the birds of the air and the beasts of the field in the natural ordering of His universe, why should He not furnish it for me in the supernatural? And if the plant nourishes its seed before it is ripe, and if the bird brings food to its young before they can fly, shall I deny to Him that which I allow to a creature? To every infant at the breast, the mother virtually says: "Take, eat, drink, this is my body given for you." And as the mother would be untrue to fact in saying of her infant's food: "This represents my body," knowing that it is her body, so too the Lord would be untrue to fact in saying: "My Flesh is meat indeed and my Blood is drink indeed," if He meant only a representation of His Body and Blood. Certainly the servant is not above the Master, and what a mother can do in the natural order, God can do and actually has done in the supernatural order. And His word I believe, for no man ever spoke as this Man. In short, shall not Christ really be a Divine Pelican which is represented as wounding its side to feed its young with its own substance?

The Eucharist is requisite by the very necessity whereby life, which has not the plenitude within itself, must nourish itself on other life. And if this be true of the body, it is ten thousand times more true of the soul, for, "What shall it profit a man if he gain the whole world and suffer the loss of his soul?"

Not only do we find an analogy for the Eucharist in the communion of life with life, but also in the very elements of nature which Christ chose as the matter of the sacrament. As if the better to remind us of His passion in the Sacrifice of the Mass, He chose bread and

wine, both of which become what they are
through a kind of Calvary. Wheat becomes
bread and grapes become wine through a
veritable passion of the grist-mill and the wine-
press. This has been well brought out in the
following lines:

"Come, dear Heart!
  The fields are white to harvest: come and see
  As in a glass the timeless mystery
  Of love, whereby we feed
  On God, our bread indeed.
  Torn by the sickles, see him share the smart
  Of travailing Creation: maimed, despised,
  Yet by his lovers the more dearly prized
  Because for us he lays his beauty down—
  Last toll paid by Perfection for our loss!
  Trace on these fields his everlasting Cross,
  And o'er the stricken sheaves the Immortal Vic-
    tim's crown.

  From far horizons came a Voice that said,
  'Lo! from the hand of Death take thou thy daily
    bread.'
  Then I, awakening, saw
  A splendour burning in the heart of things:

The flame of living love which lights the law
Of mystic death that works the mystic birth.
I knew the patient passion of the earth,
Maternal, everlasting, whence there springs
The Bread of Angels and the life of man.

Now in each blade
I, blind no longer, see
The glory of God's growth: know it to be
An earnest of the Immemorial Plan.
Yea, I have understood
How all things are one great oblation made:
He on our altars, we on the world's rood.
Even as this corn,
Earth-born,
We are snatched from the sod;
Reaped, ground to grist,
Crushed and tormented in the Mills of God,
And offered at Life's hands, a living Eucharist." [4]

The Eucharist is, among the means God
has provided mankind for working out his
salvation, one of the great needs in our modern
civilization and the cure of its ills and can-
cers. It emphasizes the great truth that we must

[4] Evelyn Underhill, "Corpus Christi."

not labor for the meat that perisheth but for the bread that endureth unto life everlasting. Just suppose that to-morrow morning every person in the world received Holy Communion. Would there be the strife between capital and labor? Would there be the wars between nations and the battle of armaments? Would our divorce courts be glutted with those who attempt to break bonds which God has joined together? Such a condition where the whole world would break its fast on the Bread of Life and the wine that germinates virgins, would be the ideal and will never be realized as long as there are wolves among sheep; but even a better approach to that ideal would work untold good in our civilization.

It is well for us to remember that civilization is capable of a twofold degeneration. The blood of man may become too cold, then we have barbarism; or it may become too hot, then we have effeminacy. Barbarism is cold-bloodedness; effeminacy is hot-bloodedness.

114

In times of barbarism man becomes like a tiger or worse than a tiger. In his wrath the animal never oversteps the limits of his instinct, but man does. Because he has a soul which is in a certain sense, infinite in its possibilities, it can communicate something of that "infinity" to the body. To-day barbarism is dead, and it is dead thanks to the civilizing influence of the Church and the Sacraments. Its death is typi-fied in Attila the Hun turned back from Rome at the very sight of the unarmed Leo the Great. But effeminacy is not dead. It is the curse of the modern world. It shows itself in a twofold way, in what we might call a degeneration of the mind, and in a degeneration of the body.

Our civilization is suffering from a degener-ation of the mind. We pride ourselves on being intellectually advanced, and yet if real culture is a knowledge of the truth, then we are less advanced than we were several centuries ago. There is such a thing as ever learning and never coming to the knowledge of the truth.

Thousands of our educated minds are dedicated to the materialist philosophy which denies that man can rise above a knowledge of earthly things. Sacred Scripture informs us that when the earth passes away there will be no more time, and yet prophets of our day teach us that the only abiding reality is space and time. Realities which cannot be touched are denied. There is said to be no spiritual soul because a scalpel never revealed it; no mysteries in life because never handled in a laboratory; no world beyond this world because never seen through a telescope. And faith, if there be any, means only a hypothesis or a sum of probabilities. Such are the tenets of a materialism, the Dead Sea fruit of a brain softening and atrophied through the misuse of its higher powers.

Besides this degeneration of the mind, there is the degeneration of the body—the second kind of effeminacy. Our body is no longer hardened to the tasks of life; we fear sacrifices and

116

efforts. We shrink from fasting, pamper our body as if it were a lasting city. Our push-buttoned, limousined, upholstered age craves for new excitements, new thrills, new shocks. We are jaded before we have come to man's estate, and the simple things of life no longer please us. A demand is made on the theater that it supply the new stimuli that will thrill. There is an overemphasis of sex in the modern life. Love and romanticism of the type of Romeo and Juliet have passed away. There is a craving for new thought, new psychology, new everything in a hectic attempt to shock and amuse. Psychology is talked of as if it were a new science. Now it is degenerated into a study of the subconscious mind—that unthinking unconscious cellar part of our mental lives—in an attempt to make us believe that we are better men when we glorify the irrational and have not our wits about us. We want our music at a distance and do not care what kind of music it is. It is the thrill of space that

117

pleases and not the thrill of culture and talent. We undergo all manner of pain, not to improve our minds or our hearts, but to preserve life which seems to have no higher function than to be the condition of a thrill. Life! Life! A more satisfying, richer, fuller life—such is the plea of the modern age.

And the remedy for this twofold degeneration—degeneration of the mind and degeneration of the body—is the Eucharist. The Eucharist is the remedy of the first because it demands faith; it is the remedy of the second, because it answers the plea for real life and youthfulness.

The faith in the Eucharist is the remedy for mental degeneration. Materialism is a foundation for a philosophy, but it is not the final philosophy of life. Spiritual truths are its complement, and faith gives the vision for these. Because the Eucharist demands faith of the right kind it is the proper therapeutic for bad thinking. And faith, be it well understood, is

118

not that sort of thing that says it is better to
call things better because they are worse; nor
does faith denounce a toothache which does
not exist for existing; nor does it tell you there
is no matter, and hence no pain; nor does it
tell you that believe that you will become a
millionaire, and you will become one. Faith
is an intellectual assent to a truth on the authority of God revealing—and is a gift of God.
We have the same eyes during the night that
we have during the day, but we cannot see at
night. Why? Because we have not the light of
the sun. So too, there are unbelievers and be-
lievers who look at the same truth—the one
sees bread, the other Emmanuel, because one
has the additional light—the light of faith.
There are three worlds in the temple of this
universe; the world of matter, the world of
spirit, and the world of grace, and they constitute respectively the vestibule, the sanctuary
and the Holy of Holies of creation. The key
that unlocks the world of matter is not the
119

same that unlocks either the world of spirit or the world of grace. God in His Wisdom has given three keys, all three of which man may possess. The key that unlocks the world of matter or the vestibule of creation is sense-knowledge, for through our senses we know the visible things of the world. The key that unlocks the world of spirit, or the sanctuary of creation, is the intellect, which can know the intimate nature of realities and can elevate itself to a knowledge of those realities which the senses never dream of; such realities as truth, goodness, virtue, justice and the source of all these, God Himself. The key which unlocks the supernatural order, the Holy of Holies, the world of grace, is the light of faith, for what sunlight is to the eye, that faith is to the reason: it is the revelation of a new kind of daylight, the daylight of the Light of the World. Faith does not impair the reason. Faith does not mean that we have to take leave of our reason. It means that we must glorify

120

it. A telescope does not destroy the vision of the eye but enables it to see objects at a distance; so too does faith perfect the reason and reveal to it a whole new field of vision which otherwise would have escaped it even with the most powerful instrument.

Faith is a mystery, but it is always the mystery which makes everything below it so clear. A celebrated essayist has compared it to the sun. The sun is the mystery of the natural order, for it is the one thing we cannot "see"; it is too bright! and yet it is in the light of the sun that everything is clear. So too, if a mystery is introduced in religion, namely something above and not opposed to reason, like the Incarnation, everything else in the world is made clear in the light of that mystery. But to try to make everything clear is like blotting out the mystery of the sun. It would be the extinction of daylight.

The Eucharist is likewise the remedy for the softening of the body. It is the unique answer to the modern appeal for life. None of these modern tendencies which we have mentioned is absolutely evil; nothing is. They are just so many aberrations of the truth; they are so many clamorings of a generation which does not know for what it is clamoring. Just as St. Paul found in the streets of Athens a statue to the unknown God and told the Athenians: "What therefore you worship without knowing it, that I preach to you." So too, the craving for life and for youthfulness, which is the craving of the modern world, is really the craving for the Eucharist. To keep young is the great desire of the age suffering from softening of the body. All wish to remain attached to that period of life that is the source of a bounding and leaping joy. But what is youthfulness? Is not youthfulness nearness to the source of life? And what is the source of our earthly life? Is it not our parents? Hence a child five years of age is younger than a child of twelve. It is seven years closer to the source of its life. A

122

man of seventy is older than a man of twenty-five. Because that man is forty-five years more distant from the source of his life, namely, his parents.

Being young then is a question of being close to the source of our life. But God is the ultimate source of life. Nothing has life but Him, for He is Life itself. It follows then that the closer we are to God the younger we become, and the further away we are from Him, the older we become. Hence I can imagine a person becoming younger as he becomes older, in other words, as he grows older in years, he grows younger by a greater union with God. This is not a useless metaphor nor mere empty verbiage. It is founded on the elementary truth that animal life is not the highest kind of life. So true is it that we become younger as we become more possessed of Divine Love, that the Church calls the day on which the saints die, their birthday: *natalitia,* for on that day they are born to the Perfect Life with God. Do we not call the day on which we are born to the imperfect life of this earth, our birthday? Why should not the Church call the day on which we are born to the Perfect Life, our birthday? The world celebrates its birthdays on the day we are born to earthly life; the Church celebrates its birthday on the day we are born to Heavenly life.

Here too is revealed the beauty of the Church's liturgy. The Church celebrates in her calendar only three birthdays to physical life: The Nativity of Our Lord, December twenty-fifth; the Nativity of the Blessed Mother, September eighth; the Nativity of John the Baptist, June twenty-fourth. And why only these three? Because their physical births were free from sin, while all others are born with the stain of sin, and hence spiritually dead. Our Divine Lord being God was absolutely sinless; the Blessed Mother was conceived free from sin, or in other words, Immaculately Conceived; and St. John the Bap-

124

tist was purified in his mother's womb during
the Visitation of the Blessed Virgin Mary.

The source of life is not far distant. It is
not necessary to travel over uncharted seas in
search of its fountain, for that Life which
passes from Father to Son in the Eternal Generation of the Blessed Trinity, from Son to
Human Nature in the Incarnation, from the
Incarnation to the Church in the Sacraments,
is the Life which passes to us in the Eucharist.

The world to-day is dying of hunger. There
is a famine on earth just as there was some
twenty centuries ago when the King of Kings
was born. This famine is a hunger for Divine
Truth in all its forms, but as if to convince
the world that among the means of salvation
one of the most wonderful was the spiritual
bread which assuaged that hunger and broke
that famine, He, "the Living Bread," was born
in the "House of Bread"—for that is the meaning in Hebrew of Beth-Lehem. It is only by
making our way back to the House of Bread

that we enjoy intimacies with Emmanuel, intimacies, which far surpass those of John listening to the throbbings of the Sacred Heart, and as we stoop to adore, we will see the continuity of Bethlehem and the altar; the stable: the first tabernacle: the manger: the first ciborium; and Christ the unique Host and Victim.

THE SECOND LAW OF LIFE: MORTIFICA-
TION

THE SECOND LAW OF LIFE—
MORTIFICATION

ALL life, it was said, must expand by nourishment. The plant must live and it feeds on the chemicals; the animal must live and it feeds on plants; man's body must live and it nourishes on plants and animals. But man has a soul and since the soul is spiritual it demands a spiritual kind of food. This food in general is Revelation and in particular, in the present order of salvation, the great gift of the Eucharist which might not have been given, but which was given that man might enjoy a more intimate communion with God.

There is yet another process of life, viz.: the katabolic, which corresponds to contraction in the mineral order. Iron not only expands when it is heated but it also contracts when it is cooled. Life not only nourishes itself but becomes the nourishment for other kinds of life. The various orders of creation are so many different expressions of this law. The plant not only consumes the hydrogen, oxygen, sunlight, and water which are necessary for its life, but in its turn becomes food for the animal; the animal not only nourishes itself on the plants of the field, but even gives its life for man in order to be served as food at his table. Once a thing has been nourished by a kingdom below, it becomes, in its turn, the nourishment of a kingdom above it. If this law did not exist all life would perish from the earth. If the chemical kingdom in a selfish way would refuse to give itself to plants, if the sky would refuse to bless the plant with its rain, all plant life would perish from the earth. If the plant in a selfish way would refuse to give its nourishment to the animal in the field; if the seed would refuse to give itself as food to the bird; if the sea would refuse to feed the fish—then all animal life would pass away from this earth. If the chemicals and the plants and the animals would refuse to give their energies and their lives for man, then all human life would pass away from this earth. In other words, life must not only expand by growing, but must die by contraction in order to become the food of a higher life. The whole universe would be a world of parasites if things did not give up their lives for other things.

But is this law of destruction and immolation just? What are its benefits?

First, is it just that life should exist for other life? We can answer this question by asking another. Has the plant life within itself? Has the animal a perfect life? Does not the very fact that plants and animals and man need nourishment prove that they have not a perfect life, but that they are dependent on other life? Only God has perfect life. If nothing has perfect life but God, shall we deny to this imperfect life the right to live? And if we admit

131

the right to live, we admit the right to live on a lower plane of life. Shall we deny reciprocity in the order of living things? Is it not just that if things nourish themselves on others, they in their turn should become the nourishment of something higher? In other words, it is only just that if things consume, they shall also be consumed; if they immolate, they shall also be immolated; if they receive, they shall also give.

What is the benefit and the purpose of all this? What high purpose could God have had in imposing this law of immolation on the actual universe? He has a most wonderful plan if we would but study it closely, and His plan is to give to each of the kingdoms a higher life than they naturally possess. The mineral kingdom, the air, the sunlight, the carbonates and the like have no life. But what happens to them once they enter into the plant? The plant does not destroy them; it does not blot out their existence; it takes away nothing either from their dignity or their rôle, but it adds

132

something to them. It ennobles the mineral by associating it with its life; it makes it share a life which it never enjoyed before. It gives the mineral new laws; it confers on it the dignity of plant life. In other words, it elevates the nature of the mineral kingdom.

The same benefit accrues to the animal kingdom. As the mineral gives itself up in order to live a higher life in the plant, so too does the plant immolate itself for the animal in order to have its life ennobled in the animal. The plant is torn up from the soil by the roots; it is plucked from the pasture by the devouring teeth of beasts; it is ground as food and passes into the animal organism. But in passing into the animal it does not cease to be plant-life; if it did it would never nourish the animal. What does happen is that it now begins to be governed by other laws directed to new purposes, organized in new cells—in a word, the plant now begins to take on a higher life, for it sees and hears and is conscious, because it is one with the animal. In other words, its nature is elevated and "reborn." This is, as it were, its reward for self-immolation.

As the plant gives its life for the animal and lives in the animal, so do both of them give their lives for man and thus live in man. And the reward for their immolation is that all three live in man with a more magnificent existence than they ever had in themselves. They die to themselves in becoming the food of man, and yet they live again in man in a new way. They fall under a new government; they become so much a part of him that it is true to say that the mineral and the plant and the animal life feel and think and will and love in him. Their existence is ennobled; their life is enriched; their faculties take on new powers. In a word, their nature is elevated. This is their reward for immolation.

But is there anything which can ennoble the existence of man? Is there anyone for whom man can die to himself in order that he might

134

have a higher kind of existence? If there were not, what a terrible world this would be! We have no right to say there is no higher life than man, any more than the rose has a right to say there is no higher life than itself. Suppose the order of the universe stopped with man. Then the plant would be higher than man for the plant could continue its existence in an ennobled way in the animal; then the animal would be higher than man for the animal could have its existence enriched in man. Certainly there must be some nature above the nature of man into which man can be assumed in order that he might be supernaturalized. There must be some higher kind of life which will be the perfection of human life in a way immeasurably superior to the perfection of plant life on an animal. And what is this life?

It is the life of God, a life infinitely distant and remote from the life of man. We have seen the different processes by which the lower creation shares in the life of the higher. But

135

when we consider that mystery, "hidden in God from all eternity," the elevation of man to be a "sharer of the divine nature," there exists nothing in creation resembling it. We may see some faint analogy in the examples already given, but they are the examples of created things. From the life of God, every creature—even the highest angel—must be forever excluded. Yet God has communicated this life, freely and gratuitously, to intellectual creatures. God could have done this wondrous thing in various possible ways, but He has revealed to us the way He has chosen. God Himself deigned to become a sharer in our humanity in order that we might share in His Divinity. Christ Our Lord is the link between us and God. Because He has a human nature He is like unto us in all things save sin; because He has a Divine Nature in the Unity of Person, He is God. The common denominator between Him and us is His human nature. This is the link between us and the life of God.

136

Now if we are to live the higher life, if we are to become incorporated into the life of God, if we are to have our life ennobled, then we must in some way enter into the life of Christ. We must become one with Him if we are to share in His life.

But how can we enter into this higher life? How can we share in the life of Christ? The answer is simple: we must follow what would appear to be a universal law. While preserving a complete distinction between nature and grace we must follow the same law the mineral follows in entering into the plant life, and the plant in entering into the animal life, namely, *we must die to ourselves*. Before the plant can live in the animal it must be torn up from its roots and pass, in a certain sense, through the jaws of death; before the animal can enter into the life of man it must pass through fire and water which constitute its Gethsemane and its Calvary. Each thing must die to itself, it must immolate itself if it is to have its life

137

perfected. Nothing is "born" to a higher life unless it be born "from above." If the plant could speak it would say to the mineral: "Unless you are born again, you cannot enter into my kingdom." If the animal could speak it would say to the plants and the minerals: "Unless you are born again, you cannot enter into my kingdom." These elevations bear a remote and imperfect analogy to our own life. Yet Christ can speak for He is the Word; He can say to man, "Unless a man be born again of water and the Holy Ghost, he cannot enter into the Kingdom of God." And that being "born again" is Baptism. Plunged in the regenerating waters of that sacrament, we die to our natural lives and begin to live spiritual lives, not as creatures, but as very children in the Family of the Trinity, whereby we have the right to call God "Father." As the plant dies and is buried to its plant life, so too, in a more eminent way "we are buried together with Christ by baptism unto death, that as Christ is risen from the dead by the glory of the Father, so we also may walk in the newness of life." [1]

Baptism then is not an arbitrary ritual; it is a law of life, a special law of the supernatural order, it is true, but a law nevertheless. God might have used some other means to effect our incorporation into His Life, but certainly the means He has chosen are consonant with the whole order in which nature works. The necessity of Baptism as a means of eternal salvation then is of Divine origin. It was Jesus Christ Himself who told us so. But it is not just a command for the mere sake of making a ritual as some in the modern world would have us believe. Looking back from its Revelation to nature, we can see all nature crying out the necessity of Baptism in the sense that it demands a death as a condition of rebirth. This

[1] "Sinful man," says St. Thomas, "is buried by baptism in the passion and death of Christ; it is as if he himself suffered and died with the sufferings and death of the Saviour. And as the passion and death of Christ have the power of satisfying for sin and all the debt of sin, the soul associated through Baptism with this satisfaction is freed from all debts towards the justice of God." Summa III, q. 69, art. 2.

139

process of dying in order to live which is initiated in us by Baptism must be continued throughout the whole Christian life, and continued throughout the whole Christian life it is mortification. It is one of the aspects of the metabolic processes of the Christian life.

"Unless the grain of wheat falling to the ground die, itself remaineth alone." The power to find life through death makes the seed nobler than the diamond. In falling to the ground it loses its outer envelope which is a restraining power of the life within it. But once this outer skin dies in the ground, then life pushes forth into the blade. So too, unless we die to the world with its vices and its concupiscences, we shall not spring forth into life everlasting. If we are to live in a higher life we must die to the lower life; if we live in the lower life of this world we die to a higher life which is Christ. To put the whole law in the beautiful paradox of Our Divine Lord: If we wish to save our life we must lose it, that is,

140

if we wish to save it for eternity, we must lose it for time; if we wish to save it for the Father's mansions, we must lose it for this dull world; if we wish to save it for perfect happiness, we must lose it for fleeting pleasure of mortality.

"The fall doth pass the rise in worth;
  For birth hath in itself the germ of death,
  But death hath in itself the germ of birth.
It is the falling acorn buds the tree,
The falling rain that bears the greenery,
The fern-plants moulder when the ferns arise.
For there is nothing lives but something dies,
And there is nothing dies but something lives,
    Till skies be fugitives,
Till Time, the hidden root of change, updries
Are Birth and Death inseparable on earth;
For they are twain yet one, and Death is Birth." [2]

Has not this been the law of Christ? Why did He come on earth? He has told us, "I am come that you may have life and have it more abundantly." But how did He give this life? He gave it by suffering and dying. He came on

[2] Francis Thompson.

141

earth to give His life for the Redemption of many. He called Himself the "Good Shepherd" and the Good Shepherd layeth down His life for His sheep. No one taketh away His life but He layeth it down of Himself. And it was fitting that He who brings salvation to all nations must needs be killed by His own people; it suits human ideas of the fitness of things that He who offers His life should be put to death; it is fitting that He who loves His enemies should be killed by His friends. It is fitting that He who said, "The Seed is the Word of God," should give His life as the seed—that is, by falling to the ground, and this He did in a very literal sense, for He fell to the ground on two great occasions and both times Life sprang up. He fell to the ground first in the Incarnation—for He was born in a cave—and the life of God was found among men. He fell to the ground again in His Passion—for He was laid in a grave—and He rose to life glorious in the immortality of His Resurrection.

142

It is the Incarnation that matters, and the only thing in the world that ever mattered. From out the thunder and lightning of Sinai a law of fear was given to the world on tablets of stone and it read: "Thou shalt not kill." From out the darkened sky of Calvary a law of love was given to the world and this time it was not written on stone but in the torn flesh of a Crucified Savior and it read: "Fear ye not them that kill the body, and are not able to kill the soul; but rather fear him that can destroy both body and soul in Hell." Then men began to understand that it is the higher life that must be conserved, and in understanding that, they gloried with Paul in the philosophy of mortification: "To die is gain."

Look not only to His life but also to His doctrine; the same law of immolation is set before us. The modern world does not take kindly to this law of mortification and yet it falls unwittingly into a queer inconsistency. There has been a great appeal on the part of present-day

143

religion for a simplified Christianity in which
there will be no more creeds and no more dogmas. It wishes to accept from the Gospel some
few truths which will prejudice no one and
so the eight Beatitudes are chosen. The modern world talks of the Beatitudes as if they
were just a kind of lecture and a very dull lecture at that, forgetful that the Beatitudes con-
tain more dogma, more mortification, more
hardships, more un-modernities than anything
else in the Gospel. The Sermon on the Mount
is just the prelude to the Drama of Calvary.
Contrast the Beatitudes with what we might
call the beatitudes of the world; the one is the
antithesis of the other. The world says:
"Blessed are the rich"; Christ says: "Blessed
are the poor in spirit." The world says:
"Blessed are the mighty"; Our Lord says:
"Blessed are the meek." The world says:
"Laugh and the world laughs with you";
Christ says: "Blessed are they that mourn."
The world says: "Be for yourself and your

country right or wrong"; Christ says: "Blessed are they that hunger and thirst after justice." The world says: "Sow your wild oats, you are young only once; blessed is the sex appeal"; Christ says: "Blessed are the clean of heart." The world says: "In time of peace prepare for war"; Christ says: "Blessed are the peacemakers." The world says: "Blessed are those who never suffer persecution"; Christ says: "Blessed are they that suffer persecution." The world says: "Blessed is popularity"; Christ says: "Blessed are ye when they shall revile you and persecute you and speak all that is evil against you for My sake."

In so many words the Sermon on the Mount placed an irreconcilable opposition between the world and Christ. He upset every maxim of the world as He upset the tables of the money-changers in the temple, and said openly that He prayed not for the world: "If the world hate you, know ye, that it hath hated Me before you. If you had been of the world, the world would love its own: but because you are not of the world, but I have chosen you out of the world, therefore the world hateth you." Every standard the world ever held He upset with a ruthless abandon. He was the Iconoclast of the world, smashing to fragments its false idols. He talked in the language of the paradox for only the paradox could express that opposition between Himself and the world. The lofty, He said, shall be brought low; the first shall be last; the overlooked shall be preferred; the scorned shall be reverenced; the needy shall possess all things; the reviled shall bless; the persecuted shall suffer patiently; the blasphemed shall entreat; the weak shall be strong; the strong shall be weak; the fool shall be wise and the wise shall be foolish. He wrote the law of Christianity by the example of His own life and that law is: The death of all things in their first stage is the necessary condition of infinite progress. Nothing is quickened unless it die.

"Could we but crush that ever-craving lust
For bliss, which kills all bliss; and lose our life,
Our barren unit life, to find again
A thousand lives in those for whom we die:
So were we men and women, and should hold
Our rightful place in God's great universe,
Wherein, in heaven and earth, by will and na-
    ture,
Nought lives for self. All, all, from crown to
    footstool
The lamb, before the world's foundation slain
The angels, ministers to God's elect;
The sun, who only shines to light a world;
The clouds, whose glory is to die in showers;
The fleeting streams, who in their ocean graves
Flee the decay of stagnant self-content;
The oak, ennobled by the shipwright's axe;
The soil, which yields its marrow to the flower;
The flower which breeds a thousand velvet worms,
Born only to be prey to every bird—
All spend themselves on others; and shall man,
Whose twofold being is the mystic knot
Which couples earth and heaven—doubly bound,
As being both worm and angel, to that service
By which both worms and angels hold their
    lives—

147

Shall he, whose very breath is debt on debt,
Refuse, forsooth, to see what God has made
  him?
No, let him show himself the creature's lord
By free-will gift of that self-sacrifice
Which they, perforce, by nature's law must suf·
  fer;
Take up his cross, and follow Christ the Lord."

Unless there is a Good Friday in our lives, there will never be an Easter Sunday; unless there is a cross, there will never be an empty tomb; unless there is the torn flesh, there will never be the glorified body. The crown of thorns is the condition of the halo of light, and every resurrection presupposes a death, as every death is the antecedent of resurrection. Unless we die to the world, we shall never live to Christ; unless we lose our life, we shall never save it. The whole cross is easier to carry than half of it; it is only its splinters and its shadows which frighten. There is no such thing as walking around the cross; the outstretched arms will not permit that—we must climb

148

over it—and the climbing over it is the crucifixion.

> "Nothing begins, and nothing ends,
>   That is not paid with moan;
>   For we are born in others' pain,
>   And perish in our own."

But what is the motive force behind this
law of immolation? What is the inspiration
of this law of dying to ourselves in order to
live to another? What mysterious energy is it
that inspired the Incarnate Word to make our
dead selves stepping stones to higher things?
It is love. Love is the inspiration of all sacrifice. And love, be it understood, is not the desire to have, to own, to possess—that is selfish-
ness. Love is the desire *to be had, to be owned,
to be possessed*. It is the giving of oneself for
another. The symbol of love as the world understands it is the circle continually sur-
rounded by self, thinking only of self. The
symbol of love as Christ understands it, is the
cross with its arms outstretched even unto

eternity to embrace all souls within its grasp. Sinful love as the world understands it finds its type in Judas the night of the betrayal: "What will you give me and I will deliver Him unto you." Love, in its true sense, finds its type in Christ a few hours later when, mindful of his disciples, he says to the friends of the traitor who blistered His lips with a kiss, "If therefore you seek Me, let these go their way."

Love then is the giving of self and as long as we have a body and are working out our salvation, it will always be synonymous with sacrifice, in the Christian sense of the word. Love sacrifices naturally just as the eye sees and the ear hears. That is why we speak of "arrows" and "darts" of love—something that wounds. The bridegroom who loves will not give to his bride a ring of tin or of brass, but one of gold or of platinum, because the gold or platinum ring represents sacrifice—it *costs* something. The mother who sits up all night nursing her sick child does not call it hardship, but love.

The day men forget that love is synonymous with sacrifice, that day they will ask what selfish sort of woman it must have been who ruthlessly extracted tribute in the form of flowers, or what an avaricious creature she must have been who demanded solid gold in the form of a ring, just as they will ask what cruel kind of God is it who asks for sacrifice and self-denial. And if there is a young lover in the world who will do anything for the one he loves, then I do not find it unreasonable that a God should so love the world as to send into it His only Begotten Son. And if a father will lay down his life for his son then I shall not find it unreasonable that the Son of God should lay down His life for His friends, "for greater love than this no man hath." Such an analogy is imperfect, for Our Lord did more than follow a mere law of nature. His love was so great, His condescension and sacrifice so great, that any attempt to make them reasonable according to the dictates of human reason must always fall short of the truth. If all lovers tend to become like those they love, then I shall not be surprised to find creatures who will lay down their lives for their Divine Lover; and who will become so much like Him that they will carry about on their body the stigmata of the Passion. Love is the reason of all immolation. So too the man who loves his perfected life in Christ will die to himself and this dying to himself, this taming of his members as so many wild beasts, this being imprinted with the cross, is mortification. Christ then has given no new law when He said that we must fall to the ground and die. He merely restated a law which our experience has verified a thousand times and still has not yet learned to apply to every corner of the universe, and particularly those corners of our souls which need it so badly.

Love, simply because it does inspire mortification, is foolishness from the world's point of view. No one ever quite understands the lovers but the lovers themselves; they live in a universe apart; they breathe another atmosphere; they do the unexpected, the unreal, the irrational—even the foolish. It is the law of love.

"The young Francis Bernardone was summoned by his father before the Bishop of Assisi for having squandered his wealth on the poor. Francis sold his own horse and then several bales of his father's cloth, making a sign of the cross over them to show their charitable destination. His father did not understand such foolishness and so he took the matter up in a legal way before the Bishop. Francis' retort was as pointed as a spear. "Up to this time," he said to his father, "I have called Pietro Bernardone father, but now I am the servant of God. Not only the money but everything that can be called his, I will restore to my father, even the very clothes he has given me." And he rent off all his garments except one—and that one was a hair shirt. He piled his garments in a heap on the floor and tossed the money on top of them. He went out half naked in his hair shirt into the winter woods, walking the frozen ground between the frosty trees—a man without a father. He was pen-

153

niless, he was parentless, he was to all appearances without a trade, or plan or hope in the world, and as he went under the frosty trees he burst suddenly into song. He made a fool of himself. It was a solid objective fact like the stones in the road that he made a fool of himself. He saw himself as an object very small and distinct like a fly walking on a clear window pane; and it was unmistakably a fool. And as he stared at the word "fool" written in luminous letters before him, the word itself began to shine. He would go on being a fool; he would become more and more of a fool; he would become so foolish that he would devour fasting as a man devours food and plunge after poverty as madly as man digs after gold; and tear at his flesh as insanely as other men pamper it. In a word, he —St. Francis of Assisi—would become the court fool of the King of Paradise." [3]

If love is equivalent to sacrifice and all sacrifice from the world's point of view is foolishness, Christ on the Cross is the supreme folly. From the standpoint of the world He was the greatest failure in history; in the ledger of the

[3] "St. Francis of Assisi," G. K. Chesterton.

world's estimate of things, He suffered the greatest defeat. First of all, He could not win and could not keep friends. Peter, His chief apostle, denied Him to a maidservant; John, who leaned on His breast, is silent when the Master is accused; Judas, whom he called to be one of the judges of the twelve tribes of Israel, sells Him for thirty pieces of silver. In His four trials, before the four judges, He failed to have a single witness to testify in His favor. He could not keep His friends and is not that the test of one's success in life?

More than that, if He were God, why did He not try to win the favor of Pilate when he said, "Know you not that I have power to release you?" He could have won his freedom by ingratiating Himself with the Roman governor, and He did not.

"Folly," cries the world.

If He is all powerful, why does He not strike dead those who scourge and mock Him?

"Folly," again cries the world.

155

If He could raise up children of Abraham from the stones, why could He not raise up friends at the moment of arrest?

"Folly," cries the world.

If He could have won His release from Herod with just a miracle, why did He not work one?

"Folly," cries the world.

If He could sustain the whole world in the palm of His hand, why did He permit Himself to fall beneath the weight of the cross?

"Folly," cries the world.

If the magic touch of His hands could restore sight to the blind and hearing to the deaf, why did He permit hard nails to pierce them?

"Folly," cries the world.

If He could have proven His divinity by coming down from the cross, "Let Him now come down from the cross and we will believe Him," why did He not step down as a King from His throne?

"Folly," cries the world.

156

As a demagogue He would have succeeded; as a God He was crucified. The cross is a folly and Christ a failure.

Hence it is that every lover of Christ and Him crucified must share His folly. The law is no different for the disciple than for the Master. The world calls everyone a fool who leaves his riches and his friends, his wine and his song, for the cloister or the convent, and exchanges his silks and satins for the hair shirt and the discipline. The world calls him a fool who does not strike back when he is struck and who does not malign when he is maligned; for is it not divine foolishness to say: "To him that striketh thee on the one cheek, offer also the other"? The world calls him a fool who follows the so-called old and "antiquated" laws of the Church on the sanctity of marriage and rejects the modern views that glorify license and lust. The world brands him as a fool who hangs himself on the cross of mortification when he might come down and shake dice with the soldiers even for the garments of a God.

Yes, but "the foolishness of God is wiser than men," and "the wisdom of this world is foolishness with God." It is only from the world's point of view that we are a fool as our Master was before the court of Herod. In the sublime words of St. Paul, "We are fools for Christ's sake." Common sense never drove any man mad; common sense is said to be sanity and yet common sense never scaled mountains and much less has it ever cast them into the sea. Common sense is not violence and yet, "the kingdom of heaven suffereth violence, and the violent bear it away." Common sense never makes a man lose his life, and yet it is in losing our life that we shall save it. Life sometimes can be saved by stepping within an inch of death in jumping a precipice, but common sense never makes the leap. The soldier at times can cut his way out from his enemies but he must have a carelessness about dying— and common sense has not that carelessness.

158

The Kingdom of Heaven can sometimes be gained only by plucking out an eye—but common sense never plucked it out. "It is common sense that makes a man die for the sake of dying," it is love which makes a man die for the sake of living—and so too, it is this love of Jesus Christ and Him crucified, which produces the wisdom of heaven at the cost of the foolishness of earth; which makes men throw down their lives to take them up again; which makes men sell fields for the pearl of great price; which makes creatures fling "the world a trinket at their wrist," laugh at death, and say with a modern saint, "I need no resignation to die but resignation to live." This does not mean the Gospel of Christ is a gospel of sorrow.

"It is but a superficial view of things to say that this life is made for pleasure and happiness. To those who look under the surface it tells a very different tale. The doctrine of the Cross does but teach, though infinitely more forcibly, the very

159

same lesson which this world teaches to those who live long in it, who have much experience in it, who know it. The world is sweet to the lips, but bitter to the taste. It pleases us at first, but not at last. It looks gay on the outside, but evil and misery lie concealed within. When a man has passed a certain number of years in it, he cries out with the Preacher, "Vanity of vanities, all is vanity." Nay, if he has not religion for his guide, he will be forced to go further, and say: "All is vanity and vexation of spirit; all is disappointment; all is sorrow; all is pain." The sore judgments of God upon sin are concealed within it, and force a man to grieve whether he will or no. Therefore the doctrine of Christ does but anticipate for us the experience of the world. . . . The Gospel hinders us from taking a superficial view, and finding a vain transitory joy in what we see; but it forbids our immediate enjoyment, only to grant enjoyment in truth and fullness afterwards. It only forbids us to *begin* with enjoyment. It only says, if you begin with pleasure you will end in pain. It bids us begin with the Cross of Christ, and in that Cross we shall at first find sorrow, but in a while peace and comfort will rise out of that sorrow. That Cross will lead us to mourning, repentance, humiliation, prayer, fasting; we shall sorrow for our sins, we shall sorrow with Christ's suffering; but all this sorrow will only issue, nay, will be undergone in a happiness far greater than the enjoyment which the world gives—though careless worldly minds indeed will not believe this, ridicule the notion of it, because they never have tasted it, and consider it a mere matter of words, which religious persons think it decent and proper to use, and try to believe themselves, and get others to believe, but which no one really feels . . . They alone are able truly to enjoy this world who begin with the world unseen. They alone enjoy it, who have first abstained from it. They alone can truly feast, who have first fasted; they alone are able to use the world, who have learned not to abuse it; they alone inherit it, who take it as a shadow of the world to come, and who for that world to come relinquish it.[4]

The apostle tells us then, not in a harsh stoic manner, that if we are to live to Christ, we must "die daily." A happy death is a masterpiece and no masterpiece was ever perfected in a day. Dubois spent seven years in making

[4] Cardinal Newman. "The Cross of Christ, the Measure of the World—Parochial and Plain Sermons."

the wax model for his celebrated statue of Joan
of Arc. One day the model was finished and the
bronze was poured into it. And the statue
stands to-day as a ravishing perfection of the
sculptor's art. In like manner our death at the
end of our natural existence must appear as a
ravishing perfection of the many years of labor
we have given over to its mould by dying daily.
The greatest reason why we fear death is because we have never prepared for it. Most of
us die only once when we should have died a
thousand times—aye, when we should have
died daily. Death is a terrible thing for him
who dies only when he dies; but it is a beautiful thing for him who dies before he dies.
There is an interesting inscription over the
tomb of Duns Scotus in Cologne which reads:
Semel sepultus bis mortuus—a double death
preceded his burial—and there is not one trav-
eler in a hundred who understands the mystery
of love behind it. After death there is no rem-

edy for an evil life, but before death there is a remedy—it is by dying to ourselves. It is by following that law of immolation which is the law of the whole universe. There is no other way of entering into a higher life except by dying to the lower; there is no possibility of man's enjoying an ennobled existence in Christ unless he is torn up from the earth. Death then never comes like a thief in the night, because it is we who take it by surprise. "We die daily in order to try dying and then again in order to succeed." Hence those who have learned to die before they die are the greatest optimists in the world. St. Lawrence was such an optimist—we might even say the patron saint of optimists—for while being roasted alive on a gridiron, in testimony of his faith, he said to his executioners with the coolness of a foolish lover of Christ, "Turn me over now, I am baked on this side." But this optimism can come only to the fools of Christ who throw away gold for thorns, palaces for crosses, gold and crimson for the red robe of scorn and begin to live with a new and maddening enthusiasm the Lover Who became a Fool that we might become wise.

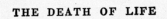
THE DEATH OF LIFE

· V ·

THE DEATH OF LIFE

ALL life that is not Life must struggle for its existence, for all living things tend toward equilibrium between the forces which build up and the forces which tear down. Life continues to exist in the individual as long as there is a balance in favor of assimilation as against dissimilation. This asserted in terms of the hierarchy of creation means that life continues just as long as a higher kingdom dominates a lower kingdom. The plant lives as long as it dominates the chemical order, not as something outside it, but as something assimilated to it; the animal lives as long as its powers dominate the chemical and plant kingdoms, and man's body lives as long as it dominates the life of these lower kingdoms.

Here again we take up a phenomenon of life so commonly known to us, and use it as an analogy to illustrate a supreme truth revealed to us by God Himself. To do so we must pass into an entirely different order, but the analogy of the natural order will continue to serve as an explanation.

It was said that life lives as long as a higher order dominates a lower order. Now man has not only a body but a soul. Each has its life. The life of the body is the soul; the life of the soul is Christ.

As long as the soul dominates the body, as long as man follows the dictates of right reason, man lives a moral existence naturally. But experience bears out what Revelation teaches, namely that man cannot keep the whole moral law over a long period of time without falling into sin. Man therefore needs help from above and aids which nature cannot supply, and this higher life which gives strength to the soul is grace. It makes us

168

children of God, partakers of the Divine
Nature, and heirs of heaven. Grace is the life
of Christ in the soul. We said before that man
lives naturally when the life of the soul
dominates the life of the body: here we add
that man lives supernaturally as long as the
life of Christ dominates the soul and through
it all nature. It is thanks to this participated
life of God in the soul through grace that even
the human body takes on a new dignity.

"Creation's and Creator's crowning good;
  Wall of infinitude;
  Foundation of the sky,
  In Heaven forecast
  And long'd for from eternity,
  Though laid the last;
  Reverberating dome,
  Of music cunningly built home
  Against the void and indolent disgrace
  Of unresponsive space;
  Little, sequester'd pleasure-house
  For God and for His Spouse;
  Elaborately, yea, past conceiving, fair,

Since, from the graced decorum of the hair,
Ev'n to the tingling, sweet
Soles of the simple, earth-confiding feet,
And from the inmost heart
Outwards unto the thin
Silk curtains of the skin,
Every least part
Astonish'd hears
And sweet replies to some like region of the spheres;
Form'd for a dignity prophets but darkly name,
Lest shameless men cry "shame!"
So rich with wealth conceal'd
That Heaven and Hell fight chiefly for this field." [1]

Grace is no mere theological abstraction void of meaning and usefulness. Grace is life—the life of God among men. It is not something which cuts an unexpected tangent across the harmony of the universe, but rather it is that which perfects the universe in its highest earthly expression, viz.: man.

A treatise on grace might be called a Supernatural Biology, for the laws of organic life

[2] Coventry Patmore.

are feeble reflections of the laws of the life of grace. The very notion of biogenesis, the law that all life must come from previous life, and can never be spontaneously generated, is a natural truth which should prepare the mind for the supernatural truth that human life can never generate Divine Life, but that Divine Life must be a gift. Only life can give life, and only Life can come from Life. *Omne vivum ex vivo* is as true of supernatural biogenesis as it is of the natural. The Life of God which is grace is a pure gift of God to which we have no right whatever. It was given to man in the first Adam, and restored to man by the merits of the second Adam, Jesus Christ.

The whole order of creation affords us an analogy of the gift-quality of grace. If a stone, say the rock of Gibraltar, should suddenly break out into bloom, it would be something transcending its nature. If a rose one day would become conscious, and see and feel and touch, it would be a supra-natural act—an act totally undue to the nature of the rose as such. If an animal would break out into a reasoning process and speak words of wisdom, it would be a supra-natural act, for it is not in the nature of an animal to be rational. So too, but in a far more rigorous manner, if man, who by nature is a creature of God, becomes a child of God and a member of the family of the Trinity, and a brother of Jesus Christ, it is a supernatural act for man, and a gift which surpasses all the exigencies and powers of his nature, even more than blooming surpasses the nature and powers of marble.[2]

Grace makes man more than a "new creature," and infinitely higher than his former condition, than an animal would be if it spoke with the wisdom of Socrates. There is nothing in all creation like that gift by which

[2] Donum gratiae excedit omnem præparationem virtutis humanae. Thomas Aquinas, Summa 1–2, q. 112, art. 3.

Gratia habitualis non solum excedit *effectivo*, ut miraculum, omnes efficientes et exigentias cuislibet naturae creatae, sed excedit *essentialiter* omnem naturam creatam et creabilem et omnes vires cognoscitivas et proinde appetitivas naturae intellectualis creatae. P. Garrigou-Lagrange, De Revelatione, Vol. 1, p. 206.

God calls man a son, and man calls God "Father." The difference between mere human life and human life rendered deiform by grace is not one of development, but of generation. The source of life in both cases is as different as human and Divine paternity. The distance which separates some minerals from the vegetable kingdom may be only a hair's breadth— but the distance which separates human life and Divine Life is infinite. "No one can pass from thence hence."

The least gift of grace, the great Thomas Aquinas tells us, is worth more than all created things.[3] All the gold and precious stones; all the mansions of earth, and all its passing joys; the power of navies; the beauty of cities; the might of nature's harmonious forces; all these are as sounding brass and tinkling cymbals compared to the worth of grace infused into a soul at the moment of its

---

[3] Bonum gratiae unius (hominis) maius est, quam bonum naturae totius universi. Summa, 1–2, q. 113, art. 9 ad 2.

incorporation into Christ. Meetings in Downing Street, conferences at the White House, League meetings at Geneva, and sessions at the d'Orsay, all these are but of ephemeral importance in an ephemeral world, compared to the meeting of the soul and Christ at the well of Baptism.

The world, in the eyes of God, is divided into two classes, the sons of men and the sons of God. All are called to be sons of God, but not all accept the gift worthily, believing that if they should take Christ as their portion, they would have naught else beside. It is to forget that the whole contains the parts, and that in Perfect Life we have the joys of finite life in an infinite degree. Both types of sons are born, the one according to the flesh, the other according to the spirit. "That which is born of the flesh, is flesh; that which is born of the Spirit, is spirit." Being born of the flesh incorporates us into the life of Adam; being born of the spirit—of waters of the Holy Ghost—incorporates us into the Life of Christ. The sons of God are twice born; the sons of men once born. The true Renaissance is in the Sons of God who are reborn, not by entering again into their mothers' wombs, "for the flesh profiteth nothing," but by being born of God, becoming thereby His children and His heirs.

The sons of God are in virtue of their sonship heirs of Heaven; they pass into their heritage at death. The sons of men are heirs only of riches which rust consumes, moths eat, and thieves break through and steal. The sons of God have within themselves the seed of glory and eternal happiness, but not so with the children of men. There is more difference between two souls on this earth, one in the state of grace, and the other not in that state, than there is between two souls, one in the state of grace in this life, and the other enjoying the eternal blessedness of Heaven. The reason is that grace is the germ of glory and some day will blossom into glory just as

175

the acorn some day will become the oak.[4] But
the soul not possessed with grace has no such
potencies in it. "Dearly beloved," says St.
John, "we are now the sons of God; and it
hath not yet appeared what we shall be. We
know that when He shall appear, we shall be
like unto Him; because we shall see Him as
He is."

One wonders why a world so much given to
the philosophy of evolution does not see the
grace of Jesus Christ as the answer to its aspi-
rations. One of the reasons why evolution is
held so highly is because of the promise it gives
for the future, and yet, all that it can give, even
in its wildest form, is the unfolding of something beneath man. But here in supernatural
biology, there is the promise and the potency
of a glory for man which exceeds even his
imagination—the potency not of becoming a
superman, but a son of God. There is no emer-

---

[4] Gratia nihil aliud est quam quaedam inchoatio gloriae aeter-
nae. Summa 2-2. q. 24, art. 3 ad 2.

gent in the whole field of evolution comparable to the "new creatures" which emerge from the Sacrament of Baptism. True greatness of life is not a push from below, but a gift from above: "I am come that you may have life and that in abundance."

When we say there is a progress in life in living by the Life of God, we do not mean that any man naturally or by his own powers is capable of meriting that Life in strict justice, or growing into it as naturally as the acorn becomes the oak. Grace and glory in heaven are related as the acorn and the oak, but not the natural and the supernatural. It is absolutely impossible for a creature to share in the Divine Life of his own power. The analogy offered, which points out the gradual progression observed in created things from a lower to a higher nature, is merely a persuasion that our elevation is neither unreasonable nor untenable by a scientific mind, but it does not offer a proof of such elevation. We cannot

177

agree that because chemicals and vegetables merge into a higher life, therefore men do also; we can only suggest that if God does elevate man to a participation in the Divine Life, He in no way destroys human nature but perfects it.[5] The greater can never come from the lesser, and this applies not only to the supernatural, but to the natural order.

Life, in the broadest terms, continues to live as long as the higher order dominates a lower order, and when the soul lives by Christ Who is Eternal, it too, lives eternally. We are immortal in the natural order because God never forgot that He made us; we are immortal, from the supernatural point of view because we live by the Immortal Christ.

Death is just the inverse of this, and it may be defined as the domination of a lower order over a higher order. The plant dies when the

[5] Fides praesupponit cognitionem naturalem, sicut gratia naturam et ut perfectio perfectibile. 1, q. 2, art. 2 ad 1. Definitum est ab Ecclesia quod non potest esse dissensio inter eos "cum ambo ab uno eodemque immutabili veritatis fonte, Deo optimo maximo, oriantur." Denz. 1449, 1706, 1817.

chemical order dominates it; a poisonous gas may kill the plant immediately, or else the slow wearing away of its tissues through the absorption of the chemical kingdom brings its death. An animal dies when a lower order, either the chemical or the vegetable, dominates it, either singly or in combination. Generally it is the slow oxidization of the organism which brings about its death. Man's body dies in much the same way. The very food which we eat, and the air which we breathe carry not only life with them, but death as well. The waste products of the food gradually poison the system and the very act of nutrition burns away slowly and surely, the organs and the tissues, until finally they succumb and waste away.

But man has not only a body but also a soul. Both body and soul have their life; the life of the body is the soul and the life of the soul is Christ. Now when does the soul die? It dies when a lower order dominates it. And what is this lower order? It is the body. When body dominates the soul; when matter dominates the spirit; when that which is base dominates what is lofty; when that which is vicious dominates that which is virtuous; when the lower dominates the higher; then the soul dies, and it is here in the moral order, that death is called *sin*. That is why the Sacred Scriptures use indifferently the terms "sin" and "death." "For, the wisdom of the flesh is death." "The wages of sin is death." A man, therefore, may be living while he is dead; he may be living physically but dead spiritually. And it is this idea of the higher life of God which was in the mind of the Apostle when he spoke of those who call themselves living but really are dead. Imagine the funeral service of a man who lived in sacramental and mystic union with Christ throughout his life. His body is dead beyond all doubt, but his soul lives, not only with natural immortality which it possesses, but with the very life of

God. Suppose a pallbearer standing near-by is in the state of sin. In the eyes of God there is more death in the pallbearer than in the corpse; it is he who really is dead and, if we were spiritually-minded, we would weep over him and chant a Requiem over his soul rather than over the departed one. The real death is not the death of the body, but the death of the soul: "And fear ye not them that kill the body, and are not able to kill the soul; but rather fear him that can destroy both soul and body in hell."

Sin then is not an arbitrary tag stuck on to our actions by the Church. Sin is a death, and in a very broad way we may say that the plant "sins" when it delivers up its higher life to a lower order; we can say that the animal "sins" in permitting its life to be dominated by either the vegetable or the animal kingdom. When we come to man, sin takes on a double aspect: it is the loss of a higher life which is a gift of God, and the domination of the lower life which is that of this world. Sin, in the true sense of the word, implies a turning away from God and a turning to a creature. Its greatest malice is that it is the death of Divine Life which is in us. A mighty giant who might crush the sun and extinguish its light would not be guilty of a crime as great as the man who would extinguish either in his own soul or the soul of another, the very Life of God. Murder of the Life of the body is nothing compared to murder of the life of the soul, and that is why sin is the crucifixion over again. The curtain never goes down on the drama of Calvary, for the Crucifixion is not merely an historical event; it is also a continuous drama, for sinners are those who are "crucifying again to themselves the Son of God, and making Him a mockery."

We sit in judgment of Christ as did Pilate, and we crucify Him as truly as the executioners. Our conscience is the courtroom of Pilate. Daily and hourly there are brought before us

Barabbas and Christ. Barabbas comes as vice, murder, blasphemy—Christ comes as virtue, love and purity. Which of the two shall be released? As often as we choose to commit a mortal sin we are saying in so many words: "Release unto us Barabbas," and as for Christ, "Crucify Him, Crucify Him." The will to sin is the judgment, and its execution is the Crucifixion. We, like Judas, sell the Master and sometimes for much less than thirty pieces of silver. We betray with a kiss, for it is always with some show of affection that we deny. Hands that are outstretched to bless, we fasten with nails; feet that sought after us in the devious ways of sin, we dig with steel; heart that panteth after us, like the hart after the fountain, we pierce with a lance. And when the Crucifixion is complete, the last nail driven and the King of Kings fastened to the gibbet of contradiction, our conscience begins to quiver as did the earth at the first Crucifixion. We grow sad and fearful

183

lest perhaps He whom we thought was *only* the son of a carpenter, may be after all, the very Son of God. And we debate as to whether we should seek repentance.[6] Why does He not run after us? Why does He not pursue us? Ah, we forget! How can hands bless that are nailed fast? How can feet which are fastened go to seek souls that are lost? How can lips which are bruised and parched speak the words of forgiveness? If we are to undo the Crucifixion, and we can undo it, it is only by working whilst we have the light, by wending our way back to that blessed company of the three types of souls ever to be found beneath the cross: Mary, Magdalene and John—innocence, penitence and priesthood. But it is so hard to go back to the scene of the Crucifixion! It so wounds our pride. It is so humiliating! Yes, but it is more humiliating to hang there!

[6] As long as we are in this life, change of heart is possible. God offers the grace of repentance. But after death, when there is no change, but the ever present "now," change of heart is impossible.

Redemption comes through humiliation. Christ came to us by humbling Himself. "He humbled Himself becoming obedient unto death; even to the death on the cross," and it is through humility we must go back to Him. We meet Him at the beginning of His life in a cave; and to enter a cave we must stoop and the stoop is humiliation; we meet Him at the end of His life carrying a cross and He asks us to carry it, and that is a humiliation. "He that humbleth himself shall be exalted."

And if we refuse the humiliation which comes with the Sacrament of Penance, we do not escape it; we defer it until the Judgment. What is Judgment? Judgment may be considered both from God's point of view and from our point of view.

From God's point of view Judgment is a recognition. Two souls appear before the sight of God in that split second after death. One is in the state of grace, the other is not. The Judge looks into the soul in the state of

185

grace. He sees there a resemblance of His nature, for grace is the participation in Divine Nature. Just as a mother knows her child because of the resemblance of nature, so too, God knows His own children by resemblance of nature. If they are born of Him, He knows it. Seeing in that soul His likeness, the Sovereign Judge, Our Lord and Savior Jesus Christ says unto it: "Come ye blessed of My Father. I have taught you to pray, 'Our Father.' I am the natural Son; you, the adopted son. Come into the Kingdom I have prepared for you from all eternity."

The other soul, not possessing the family traits and likeness of the Trinity, meets an entirely different reception from the Judge. As a mother knows that her neighbor's son is not her own, because there is no participation in her nature, so too, Jesus Christ, seeing in the simple soul no participation of His nature, can only say those words which signify non-

186

recognition, "I know you not," and it is a terrible thing not to be known by God!

Such is Judgment from the Divine point of view. From the human point of view, it is also a recognition, but a recognition of unfitness or fitness. A very distinguished visitor is announced at the door, but I am in my working clothes, my hands and face are dirty. I am in no condition to present myself before such an august personage and I refuse to see him until I can improve my appearance. A soul stained with sin acts very much the same when it goes before the judgment seat of God. It sees on one hand His Majesty, His Purity, His Brilliance, and on the other its own baseness, its sinfulness, its unworthiness. It does not entreat nor argue, it does not plead a case—it *sees;* and from out the depths comes its own judgment, "Oh, Lord, I am not worthy." The soul that is stained with venial sins casts itself into purgatory to wash its baptismal robes, but the soul irremediably stained—the soul *dead* to Divine Life—casts itself into Hell just as naturally as a stone which is released from my hand falls to the ground.

Casts itself into Hell! But is there a Hell? The modern world no longer believes in it. True it is that many of our present-day prophets deny Hell, and that makes us ask the reason of the denial. The reason is probably psychological. There are two possible orientations for a man. Either he must adapt his life to dogmas, or he must adapt dogmas to his life. "If we do not live as we think, we soon begin to think as we live." If our life is not regulated in accordance with the Gospel, then the thought of Hell is a very uncomfortable kind of thought, To ease my conscience, I must deny it. I must suit a dogma to my mode of life. And this is borne out by experience. Some believe in Hell, fear it, hate it, and avoid sin. Others love sin, deny Hell but always fear it.

But granted that such be the reason for its

denial, these same prophets will ask how do you know there is a Hell. Very clearly, because Jesus Christ said there was. Either there is a Hell or Infinite Truth is a liar. I cannot accept the second proposition, so I must accept the first. But in doing so, I do no violence to my reason. That there is a Hell seems clear to me from a very evident application of one of the laws of physics; viz: for every action there is always a contrary and equal reaction. If I stretch a rubber band two inches, it will react with a force equal to two inches. If I stretch it six inches, it will react with a force equal to six inches.

Now sin is an action. It is an action against an order, and for that reason it is called a de-ordination. There are three orders against which one may act in sinning; first, the order of individual conscience; second, the order of the union of consciences or the state; and third, the source of both, God. If I sin against the first order, or my conscience, there is a reaction which is remorse of conscience, and which in normal men varies in proportion with the gravity of the sin committed. If I sin against the second order, or the state, there is a reaction in the form of a fine or an imprisonment or death. And the punishment is never meted out according to the length of time required to commit the crime, but according to the nature of the crime itself. It may take only a second to commit a murder and yet the state will take away life for such a crime. Lastly, if I sin against the third order, or the Source of all order, and I do this in sinning against any of the orders, I am acting against something Infinite. But for every action there is always a contrary and equal reaction. There will, therefore, be an infinite reaction, and an infinite reaction from God is infinite separation from God, and an infinite separation from God Who is Life, and Truth and Love, is Hell.[7]

[7] Human reason unaided by Divine Revelation possibly could never prove the existence of eternal punishment. Reason does suggest, however, the necessity of an eternal sanction for good and evil.

Why should we deny that God will allow the soul to be visited with iniquities which it brought upon itself when nature itself testifies to it. Prisons, asylums, and hospitals are courts of justice where nature is squaring its accounts with sin. There is a judgment there though no Judge is visibly seated in judgment.

Heaven and Hell are not mere afterthoughts in the actual Divine Plan. God did not, by a second act of His Will and Omnipotence, create Heaven and Hell to reward and punish those who lived according to His Divine Law. They are not arbitrary decrees, mere things to patch up an original plan disturbed by sin. No law can exist without sanction and the sanction is one with the law and bound up with it as an effect to a cause. If there were no Hell in the present order of salvation what would be the consequence? It would mean that whatever evil we did, and regardless of how long we did it, and the hatred with which we did it, God would all the while be indifferent to our moral acts, which is another way of saying that Law is indifferent to lawlessness.

All our misconceptions concerning Heaven and Hell are founded on our inability to see how they are bound up necessarily with our acts in the moral order. There are many who regard Heaven only as an arbitrary reward for a good life, a kind of token in appreciation of our victory, as a silver loving cup is awarded to the winner of a race. Such is not the whole truth. Heaven is not related to a good Christian life in the same way a silver cup is related to the winning of a race, for the silver cup may or may not follow the victory; it is not something inseparably bound up with it— something else might be given or perhaps nothing at all. Rather, Heaven is related to a Christian life as learning is related to study, that is why theologians call grace the "*seed* of glory." If I study I acquire knowledge by that very act; the two are inseparable, one being the fruition of the other. And in this connection it is well to remember that Heaven in the present constitution of God's world is not just merely a reward, it is in a certain sense, a "right," the right of heirs, for we are heirs of the Kingdom of Heaven in virtue of the gift of Divine Adoption into the sonship of God by a Heavenly Father.

Hell too, is often explained too exclusively in terms of arbitrariness. It is made to appear as a kind of punishment wholly unrelated to a life of sin and the abandonment of the gift of God. Hell is not related to an evil life as a spanking is related to an act of disobedience, for such a punishment need not necessarily follow the act. Rather Hell is bound up with an evil life in precisely the same way as blindness is related to the plucking out of an eye. If I lose my eye I am blind necessarily, and if I rebel against God, refuse His pardon, and die in sin, I must suffer Hell as a consequence. There is equity in human law, and there is equity in the Divine Law. A sin involves first a turning away from God, second, a turning to creatures. Because of the first element, the sinner suffers the Pain of Loss, or the deprivation of the Beatific Vision. Because of the turning to creatures, the sinner suffers the Pain of Sense, which is a punishment by created things for the abuse of created things, and this is commonly referred to as "hell-fire." The difference between the Pain of Loss and that of Sense consists in that the former is caused by the absence of something, the latter by the presence of something. Of the two pains the first is the more terrible, for it is the final and never ceasing frustration of the craving of an immortal being; it is the missing of the goal of life; it is the having failed so utterly as never to admit of another start; it is to want God and yet hate oneself for wanting Him; it is an asking never to receive, a seeking never to find, a knocking at a gate eternally closed; it is, above all, a void created by the absence of the Life, the Truth and Love which the soul eternally craves. How eagerly souls yearn for life; how tenaciously they cling to even a straw to save from drowning! How they desire to prolong life even into eternity! What must it be then to miss, not a long human life, but the very Life of all Living! It is a kind of living death, like the waking up in a sepulcher. Truth too, is the desire of souls. Knowledge is a passion, and the human deprival of it is pain, as is so forcibly brought home to us when we are deprived of the knowledge of a secret in which others share. What must it be then to be deprived not of an earthly truth, not something which we could learn later on perhaps, but of the Truth, outside of which there is no truth or knowledge or wisdom? It would be worse than an earthly life without sun or moon, a kind of cavernous darkness in which one moves knowing that he might have known the light of truth but would not. Finally, how dull an earthly life would be without the affection or without the love of parents, brothers, sisters and friends! How heavy our hearts would be if every other heart turned to stone! Then what must it be to be deprived of Love without which there is no love? It is to have one's heart stolen and still be able to live without it.

"The mind is darkened and the will perverted. Those whose work brings them to study the psychology of sin come across many cases of such incipient perversion even on earth. Final perversion is only an intensification, a fixing of a state by no means unknown here. The drunkard drinks, and inwardly curses himself for drinking. The debauchee wallows in sin, and detests himself for his loathsome cravings. The angry man smites in the moment of his anger, yet his own nature cries out while he strikes his friend. His cravings, his passions, his furies are upon him, they cling to him. Their grasp is more than an outward grip, they hold his will by inward compulsion. Sometimes in impotent remorse he cries out: 'My tastes are foul, my desires are loathsome; I am a cruel beast, I know it, but I cannot, I will not change; I am what

196

I am.' When a friend or a priest comes and puts the horror of his conduct before him, he fiercely faces them: 'You can tell me nothing I do not know. Preach to me, Man, I preach to myself every hour of the day, and then laugh in despair at my own eloquence! Matters have gone too far, I am what I am, better leave me alone!' [8]

"It is difficult for us to understand that anyone should hate God. The perversity seems too monstrous; no one can hate the Infinite Good. The answer to this difficulty, however, is not far to seek. If the infinite Good were directly perceived by the damned soul, he could, of course, not hate It. The fact is that the mind of the damned is darkened; though they are in eternity, they do not see God as He is. However vivid their imagination, however keen the realization of His presence, it is indirect. It is still by reason and not by an act of intuitive intelligence that they perceive Him. As such He becomes an object of their hatred and detestation because He stands in the way of what they want, what they have chosen by a final act of personal choice. He is their supreme antag-

[8] "Eternal Punishment," J. P. Arendzen, p. 18.

onist. Of a friend they have made a foe. Not that God has changed, but they have changed. They have perverted themselves.

"Now it must not be thought that the drunkard for all eternity will want drink, or the sexual sinner debauch, or the angry man eternal strife. In the changed conditions of the Hereafter the precise objects of their choice will, indeed, differ. Alcohol has no attraction probably for a disembodied soul, nor women nor vulgar brawling. But what underlies these vices is the inordinate desire of self, self-gratification, self-exaltation, of whatever kind it may be. All sin is self-seeking as opposed to God-seeking. Any particular vice indulged in on earth is only a manifestation of the preference of self before God. This self-seeking remains in the damned, and it is the very core of their damnation. The true centre of all things is God, but they are self-centred. The supreme happiness we know is love, but love means to love someone else. To love God is the supreme act of altruism which is rewarded by true happiness, because the Divine Other-One is infinitely good, and to possess infinite good is infinite happiness. The damned can love no more and therefore they are damned. Hell is the home of incurables. The dis-

198

ease that is beyond cure is their egoism. It is incurable because they everlastingly reject the only remedy that could heal them: the love of Some One Else instead of themselves." [9]

Heaven and Hell are the natural and inseparable results of acts good and bad in the supernatural order. This life is the springtime; judgment is the harvest. "For what things a man shall sow, those also shall he reap. For he that soweth in his flesh, of the flesh also shall reap corruption. But he that soweth in the spirit shall reap life everlasting."

Why do souls go to Hell? In the last analysis, souls go to Hell for one great reason, and that is—they refuse to love. Love pardons everything except one thing—refusal to love. A young man loves a maiden. He makes known his affection toward her, showers her with gifts, bestows on her more than the ordinary share of the courtesies of life, but his love is repulsed. Keeping it pure, he pursues, but all in vain;

[9] "Eternal Punishment," p. 21.

she turns a deaf ear to his wooing. Love, so long denied and cast aside, suddenly reaches a point where it will cry out: "All right, love can do no more, I am through now; we are finished." It has reached the point of abandonment.

God is the Divine Lover. As Hound of Heaven He is continually in pursuit of souls. Way back in the agelessness of eternity He loved us with an Eternal Love. When time begins for an individual soul, He gives it the riches of nature, calls it to be an adopted son, feeds it on His own substance and makes it an heir of Heaven. But that soul may soon forget such goodness, and yet God does not forget to love. He pursues the soul, sends discontent deep into it to bring it back to Him, cuts purposely across its path to manifest His presence, sends His ambassadors to it, lavishes it with medicinal graces and still Divine Love is spurned. Finally rejected more often than seventy times seven, Divine Love abandons the pursuit of such a soul which turns from Him at the end of its lease in life and cries out: "It is finished. Love can do no more." And it is a terrible thing not to be loved, and most of all not to be loved by Love. That is Hell. Hell is a place where there is no love.

LOVE

So strong that heaven, could love bid heaven fare-
    well,
Would turn to fruitless, unflowering Hell;
So sweet, that Hell, to Hell could love be given,
Would turn to splendid and sonorous heaven.[10]

And it may be asked: How can an infinitely Good God, how can He Who came on earth to forgive sinners, Who raised up Magdalene and looked kindly on Peter, how can He Who is Love itself send souls to hell? Oh, answer me this question: *How can the sun which warms so gently, also wither; how can the rain which nourishes so tenderly, also rot?*

[10] "Tristram," Swinburne.

THE HYMN OF LIFE

THE HYMN OF LIFE

THE universe reveals the profound truth that all things, from the grain of sand on even to the angels, are singing a beautiful hymn of life to the Creator. This hymn has many verses, each one more beautiful than the preceding, and all leading up to a climax in man in the natural order and to Christ in the supernatural. All life reveals itself as a process of unification. To make unity out of multiplicity; homogeneity out of heterogeneity; the same out of the different; the permanent out of the passing—that is the fundamental movement of life. This world would be like a gigantic puzzle-picture if there were no unifying force to put the pieces together. A mosaic is unintelligible if it is seen only in its details, but it takes on a new beauty when seen in its unity. The Mosque of Omar in Jerusalem has the magnificent beauty of its tinted windows ruined by the folly of petty lines running in crazy-fashion about the walls. They lead nowhere; they are like blind leaders of the blind —there is nothing to unify them. Life is beautiful only when it is reduced to unity.

The plant unifies the chemicals; the animal unifies the plants and chemicals; man unifies all three. The chemical finds its existence perfected in the plant; the plant finds its existence perfected in the animal, and the animal finds its existence perfected in man. Those things which are separated in the lower kingdom are united in the higher. The kingdom which is above subsists through that which is below, and that which is below exists to serve that which is above. As the servant serves the master, so in the hierarchy of creation the mineral serves the plant, the plant serves the animal, and all three serve man. Each exists for the other and all exist for man. Man, the "paragon of animals," combines the perfections of them all. He has the existence of the stone, the life of the plant, the consciousness of the animal, and his own peculiar perfection, intellect and will. Imagine this unification working itself out this way. Picture four vases—one of clay, another of brass, another of silver, and another of gold. Suppose the contents of the first poured into the second, the second into the third, and the third into the fourth, the golden vase, and you have some idea of the manner in which chemical, plants and animals gradually unify themselves in man. The universe is like a pyramid gradually reaching to a point at the base of which is the mineral or chemical kingdom and the peak of which is man.

All things point to man and seem to tend towards him, but not by chance or accident. Everything tends towards him because everything was made for him. But why should the whole universe wait on man, and why should it be his footstool? By what right does he lord over all that he surveys? Man rules the universe in virtue of a Divine Gift. The Magna Charta over Creation was given him in the Garden of Paradise when God said to him: "Increase and multiply and fill the earth and subject it and rule over the fishes of the sea and the birds of the air and all living things which move upon the earth. I give to you every herb bearing fruit upon the earth and all trees which have in themselves a seed of their kind—all are yours to eat, and all the birds of heaven and all things which move upon the earth and in which there is a living soul." It was the consciousness of this lordship over the universe which prompted David the prophet to cry out: "What is man that thou shouldst be mindful of him? or the son of man that thou shouldst visit him? Thou hast made him a little less than the angels; Thou hast crowned him with glory and with honor and hast set

208

him over the work of Thy hands. Thou hast subjected all things under his feet, all sheep, all oxen, moreover the beasts also of the fields, the birds of the air, and the fishes of the sea that pass through the paths of the sea." It is not because man is mightier than the mineral or the animal, that he may dominate and rule these things; as a matter of fact, he is not mightier. The lightning can kill him—but man knows that he is being killed. In other words, it is thanks to the Divine Mandate to his immortal soul that man exercises dominion over all creation. It is by right and not by might. He has a higher kind of life and hence may subdue all things unto himself. The world is his:

"Nothing hath got so far
But Man hath caught and kept it as his prey;
His eyes dismount the highest star;
He is in little all the sphere;
Herbs gladly cure our flesh, because that they
Find their acquaintance there.

209

The stars have us to bed,
Night draws the curtain, which the sun withdraws;
Music and light attend our head,
All things unto our flesh are kind
In their descent and being; to our mind
In their ascent and cause.

Each thing is full of duty;
Waters united are our navigation;
Distinguished, our habitation;
Below, our drink; above, our meat;
Both are our cleanliness. Hath one such beauty?
Then how are all things neat!

More servants wait on Man
Than he'll take notice of: in ev'ry path
He treads down that which doth befriend him
When sickness makes him pale and wan.
Oh mighty love! Man is one world, and hath
Another to attend him.

Since then, my God, Thou hast
So brave a palace built, O dwell in it,
That it may dwell with Thee at last!
Till then afford us so much wit,
That, as the world serves us, we may serve Thee,
And both Thy servants be." [1]

[1] "Man," George Herbert.

The dominion over nature has been a slow process for man. It has become particularly rapid in the last two centuries. As a matter of fact, there has been more mechanical progress in the last two hundred years than there has been heretofore in the whole history of the world, and there has been probably among the masses less spiritual progress in that period than at any other time, for prosperity does not necessarily imply progress in the paths of God. Mechanical progress is a sign of worldliness, as spiritual progress is a sign of other-worldliness. But whatever one's opinion be on this point, the fact is that man is more and more subduing the universe and bringing all things under his domination. New continents are explored; seas traversed in every sense; their currents studied; the mysteries of heaven unveiled; the course of the stars measured; their constitution analyzed; light imprisoned and made the designers of scenes; electricity harnessed to carry our thoughts from one continent to another; and the air conquered with wings of steel. The forces of nature which at so many times seemed beyond the control of man, are now unified and harnessed and directed to his own purposes. And the pity of it all is that an ungrateful world, forgetful that God whispered these hidden secrets to man, cries out: "a conflict between religion and science!" How could there be a conflict since God is the source of both? How could science be an enemy of religion when God commanded man to be a scientist the day He told him to rule over the earth and subject it? The truth is that men praised God for nature far more before the age of scientific discoveries; now they glorify man's ingenuity rather than the bounty of God.

The fact is man is king of the visible universe and all things were created for him. "All are yours." But what was God's plan in creating all things for man? Certainly not mere egotistical domination, for this would have been a deformity in the Divine Plan. God gave man the whole of visible creation on condition that he exercise in the name of all creation a threefold sacred office—that of priest, pontiff, and king. Its priest: to give to God all the sacred things a creature can give to a Creator; its pontiff: to be a bridge between the finite and the infinite; its king: because the lord and master of all visible creation. All things were made by God but not all things can speak. The mineral hidden in the bowels of the earth has no tongue; the plant has no other voice than its flower; the animal has no other language than a cry. Being dumb they need a spokesman. Their voices would have fallen at the door of the eternal mansion, if man did not transform their mute gaspings into his own language, and give them the imprint of his intelligence and his love. What joy does a conqueror receive from the smiling valleys which he has won unless he hears from a thousand throats a "Viva" in his honor? What joy would God receive, humanly speaking, from the minerals, the plants and the animals unless there was an intelligent act of gratitude? Hence it is that God has given man the power to unite all things within himself, by his intellect, in order that he might be spokesman of the world; that he might know the world, admire for the world, speak for the world, adore for the world, render thanks for the world, pray for the world, and like the three youths in the fiery furnace, sing a living Benedicite to the Creator of the world! If the mineral could speak it would thank God for its existence; if the plant could speak it would thank God for its life; if the animal could speak it would thank God for its sentiency; but man can speak, and it is in the name of all these things beneath him he must speak thanks to God. Such is the noble office of man, the spokesman of all creation! Such is his high destiny!

The universe is a great sacrament. A Sacrament in the strict sense of the term is a material sign used as a means of conferring grace, and instituted by Christ. In the broad sense of the term everything in the world is a sacrament inasmuch as it is a material thing used as a means of spiritual sanctification. Everything is and should be a stepping stone to God: sunsets should be the means of reminding us of God's beauty as a snowflake should remind us of God's purity. Flowers, birds, beasts, men, women, children, beauty, love, truth, all these earthly possessions are not an end in themselves, they are only means to an end. The temporal world is a nursery to the eternal world, and the mansions of this earth a figure of the Father's heavenly mansions. The world is just a scaffolding up which souls climb to the kingdom of Heaven, and when the last soul shall have climbed through that scaffolding, then it shall be torn down and burnt with fervent fire, not because it is base, but simply because it has done its work.

215

Man therefore partly works out his salvation by *sacramentalizing the universe;* man sins by refusing to sacramentalize it, or, in other words, by using creatures as selfish ends rather than God-ward means. Manichæism is wrong because it considers matter as an evil instead of a "sacrament." Epicureanism is wrong because it considers pleasures as a God, instead of a means to God. Sacramentalizing the universe ennobles the universe, for it bestows upon it a kind of transparency which permits the vision of the spiritual behind the material. Poets are masters in sacramentalizing creation for they never take anything in its mere material expression; for them things are symbols of the divine. Saints surpass poets in that gift, for saints see God in everything, or better, see God through everything. The poor, the lame, the blind to them are transparent like a window-pane; they are revelations of Christ as Christ Himself told us they really were: "I was sick and you visited Me." In the

216

words of a modern poet who has understood
the sacramental character of the universe:

"I see His blood upon the rose
  And in the stars, the glory of His eyes,
  His body gleams amid eternal snows,
  His tears fall from the skies.

I see His face in every flower,
  The thunder and the singing of the birds are but
      His voice—
  And carven by His power
  Rocks are His written words.

And pathways by His Feet are worn,
  His strong heart stirs the ever-beating sea,
  His crown of thorns is twined with every thorn,
  His cross is every tree." [2]

Why should man be bound to the office of
holding commerce with God? Why should not
man be independent of God? Man could not
be independent of God any more than a ray
of sunlight could be independent of the sun.
The absolute independence of the ray would

[2] Joseph Mary Plunkett.

mean its destruction, for it is only by being dependent on the sun that it survives. So it is with man in his relation with God. Let us make this clear by an example. If I should invent some great machine which would not only shorten human labor but add great material benefit to mankind, the government would give me patent rights on that invention. The rights would entitle me to all returns on my invention and would protect me against illegal encroachments of others. Now, we are "God's invention." Being His invention He has "rights" on us, which means that He is entitled to the service of our intellect and our will, and it is this service which constitutes the true perfection and liberty of man and the foundation of all religion. In other words, God is entitled to our worship for the same reason every author is entitled to a royalty on his book —it is his creation.

If man is that by which all visible creation

is unified, should there not be someone who will unify all men into a brotherhood under a common Father? If man is the king of all visible creation shall not man have a King? If man is lord and master of all that he surveys, and if everything that has not perfect life within itself, finds its perfection in a higher life, is it not fitting that man have a Lord, a Master, and King in Whom he will find his perfection?

All creation belongs to man by a Divine concession, and all men belong to Jesus Christ for a twofold reason: first, because He is King by Divine Right, born of an Eternal Father: "The Father loveth the Son and He hath given all things unto His Hand." He "is set above all principality and power and virtue and every name that is named, not only in this world but in that which is to come; and He hath subjected all things under His feet." It is in His Son, Jesus, that God has resolved to "reëstablish all things," or rather, according to the Greek text, "to gather together all things under Christ, as under only one Head."

But Christ is Our King, for a second reason, and that is, because He has conquered us from sin. There were four elements which contributed to our fall: a disobedient man, Adam; a proud woman, Eve; a tree, and the fruit of a tree. Now, only God in His sweet revenge can use the instruments of ruin as the instruments of reparation, and in His Supreme Wisdom He chose the same four: an obedient man, Christ; a humble virgin, Mary; a tree, the cross; the fruit of the tree, Christ and the Eucharist.

We are Christ's because this mighty King— King not only by Divine and Eternal Birth, but King also by conquest—won us to Himself at the battle of Calvary, the site whereon took place the only real struggle for existence. It was a struggle; it was more—a battle; a battle fought not with spitting steel but with dripping blood; a battle waged not with five stones as David waged war against Goliath, but with five wounds—hideous scars on hands and feet and side; a battle in which the armor was not steel glistening under a noon-day sun, but flesh hanging like purple rags under a darkened sky; a battle whose cry was not "Crush and kill," but "Father, forgive them, for they know not what they do"; a battle that was won not by saving a Life, but by giving It —a strange battle in which "He who slew the foe, lost the day." The cross is the Throne of the King of Kings; His blood is His royal purple; His crucifixion is His installation—and He, the King of Kings, reigns from the sign of contradiction!

As all creation revolves about man, so too, man revolves about Jesus Christ. Man is the pivot about which the whole order of nature swings; Jesus Christ is the pivot about which all supernature swings. This is the point to which we must ever recur, for without Christ this world of ours loses its intelligibility and meaning.

The modern world is vainly digging up the earth in searching for the Missing Link, when it should be digging up the soil of Calvary. We should seek the Link: not the link which is to bind us to the beast, but the link which is to bind us to God. Our family tree does not look the more beautiful because there is a beast hanging in it. The real family tree—the Tree of the whole human family—is the Cross, and Jesus Christ is the Link—because He alone binds us to God. Man is finite; God is infinite. Nothing finite can be the bridge between the two. In the event that God demands a satisfaction proportionate to the sin—for the finite has nothing in common with the Infinite— nothing infinite can be the balanced bridge, because it has nothing in common with the finite. The link must be something finite and infinite, and this is Jesus Christ, Our Lord—finite in

His Human nature, infinite in His Divine, and one in the Unity of His Person.

There are hundreds of theories to-day which attempt to account for the origin of man and the secret force that gives him dignity and precedence over lower creation. All of them, in the ultimate analysis, are reducible to two. One theory makes the dignity of man consist in a thrust from below; the other makes it consist in a gift from above. The one looks to protoplasm and cosmic forces, the other to God and Divine Grace. The first explanation can look forward only to a progeny of the children of men; the second can look forward to a progeny of the children of God. The one looks back to the earth as the source of man, the other looks up to heaven. For those whose eyes see no further than the first vision of the universe, all the trees of the forest bear only the burden of leaves; for those who are gifted with a deeper vision, all the other trees of the forest bear the burden of penitent thieves. When a man dies, for the earthly-minded, not even the leaves chant a requiem; when a man dies, for the heavenly-minded, even the earth yawns and gives up its dead. Both outlooks point to a tree, for it is the tree that matters now as in the beginning, when man balanced a fruit against a garden. *Qui in ligno vincebat, in ligno quoque vinceretur.* Man fell by a tree, it is fitting that he be redeemed by a tree, for a tree is the crux of the whole philosophy of the universe, and the crux is the Cross.

> "Crux fidelis, inter omnes arbor una nobiles:
> Nulla silva talem profert
> Fronde, flore, germine.
> Dulce lignum, dulces clavos,
> Dulce pondus sustinet."

Jesus Christ then, is the King of Kings whether or not the rabble murmurs, "we will not have this man rule over us." If He will not be King by Love now, He will be King by Justice in His Second Advent. "The Peace of

224

Christ in the Reign of Christ" must replace the
apostasy of nations and the wanderings of individuals who have forsaken the fountains of
living water, and dug for themselves cisterns,
broken cisterns that can hold no water.

"Jesus Christ must reign. But how? Jesus Christ
reigns in the intelligence by His Doctrine. He
reigns in hearts by charity; He reigns in the human
life by the observation of His laws and the imita-
tion of His virtues. He reigns in the family, con-
stituted by the Sacrament of matrimony, when it
is considered as a holy and inviolable institution,
when the authority of the parents represents that
of God from Whom it flows, when the obedience of
children is like that of the Infant Jesus, and when
all his conduct is inspired by the examples of the
Holy Family of Nazareth. Finally, He reigns in
society when it renders to God the supreme hom-
age which is due Him; when authority recog-
nizes in Him its origin and the norm of its
conduct." [3]

Does God's plan begin to unfold itself?
Does it not become increasingly clear that as

[3] Encyclical of Holy Father Pius XI, Ubi Arcano Dei.

man is king of creation, so Christ is the King of Kings? As all things exist for man, so all men exist for Christ. How elated was the soul of Newton when he discovered the laws of gravitation! He perceived little stars revolving about still greater stars, and these, in their turn, revolving about still greater ones, and then perceiving the whole vault of the heavens, he suspected that the whole solar system gravitated about another. There was no isolation in the heavens. The millions of stars that peopled the evening skies as so many tapers "lit about the day's dead sanctities," were not strewn by careless hands, but were put there with a marvelous law—and the whole world rejoiced with Newton. But here is unfolded a law of gravitation still more sublime. As all creation moves toward man, so man moves toward creation's Creator. The pyramid of creation which before rose no higher than man, now mounts up even until it pierces the very vault of heaven for the God-Man crowns it.

226

The world with Christ takes on a new character. It becomes a great "sacrament"—a material thing used as a means of spiritual sanctification. Instead of an end, it becomes a means to an end; the visible becomes the ladder by which we mount up into the invisible, and matter becomes the stepping stone to the spiritual. The world is not destined to survive. And when the day of days comes, when the sun will no longer be needed because the Word will be the Light, then Thou, O Jesus Christ, Who has been made to love the Father as no other creature has ever loved Him, will carry all men, all spirits back to Him, and as Man, Thou shalt depose at the feet of Thy Father the spoils of victory and relinquish sovereignty, and "God shall be all in all." Then will be fulfilled the prayer: "Father, that they may be one as We also are."

Such is the Hymn of Life: "All are yours, you are Christ's and Christ is God's." The whole universe is a marvelous crescendo of

perfection reaching from the atom up to man:
an immense chain linked together as measures
of music are linked on to others to ravish the
soul with the beauty of the whole. This is the
kind of progress that has scope and dignity.
This is the progress which stops not with man,
but with God; a progress which does not ex-
pect that man shall act like a beast because
he came from one, but rather that he shall act
like God because he is made to His image and
likeness; this is the kind of progress that seeks
the link with the divine not in the dry lime
of an animal kingdom, but on the rocky hill of
the place called Golgotha; this is the kind of
progress which embraces not inanimate matter
and brute life only, but matter and spirit, the
finite and the infinite; this is the kind of progress which sees the whole material world
summed up in the immaculate body of
Christ, and the human and angelic world
summed up in His soul; a progress which sees
orbs and brotherhoods of orbs interlaced in

Christ, touch the Divinity by the bonds of Hypostatic Union—indissoluble bonds, stronger than love, stronger than time, stronger than death; this is the progress which understands why He died suspended between heaven and earth, because He was the Pontifex between the two; this is the kind of progress which always has its eyes cast on a tree, where it sees man not in the terrible shape of a beast, but God in the lacerated form of man, redeeming a world that at His birth would give Him only a manger, and at His death a stranger's grave.

> "My God, what is a heart,
> That Thou shouldst it so eye, and woo,
> Pouring upon it all Thy art,
> As if Thou hadst nothing else to do?"

It remains now, before concluding, to show just how God is the end, not of the world in general, but of each and every individual heart.

There are three fundamental inclinations or tendencies in the life of every human being.

He who takes the leisure to lay his heart in a crucible to distill its yearnings will find that his fundamental cravings are for life, for truth, and for love. Riches, pleasures and honors—all of these are subordinated to something more fundamental; riches, for example, are desired merely because they can intensify the joy of living.

The first deep-rooted yearning in the human heart is the yearning for life. Of all our treasures, it is life that we surrender last, and with the most reluctance. Titles, joys, and riches, all of these go first, for all are but ministers to life. Even the very instinct which impels a man to put out his hand ahead of him when walking in the dark, proves that he is willing to injure or lose his hand rather than endanger or lose his life.

The second fundamental inclination which burns in every human breast is the desire to know truth. Every child is an incipient philosopher. One of the first questions of a child in the dawning moments of consciousness is the question "Why?" As children, we tear apart our toys to find out what makes the wheels go around. As grown-ups we never lose that desire to know the "why" and "wherefore" of things, and we tear apart, by our mental analysis, the very toy of the universe to find out what makes its wheels go around. As our body cries out for food, our soul cries out for truth, for it is as bread to the hungry and no one can live without it.

The third fundamental inclination of human nature is the desire to love and be loved. From the first day in the Garden of Eden, when God said, "It is not good for man to be alone," on even to the crack of doom, man has thirsted and will thirst for love. As a child, it is the mother who satisfies that yearning; later on, it is true companions to whom one can "unpack his heart with words"; later on, it is in the sacrament of matrimony that one finds another who shares a common life that burns itself out in loving the fruit of that common union. Love is a demand of our nature.

But do we find existence, truth and love in their plentitude on this earth? Do we carry within ourselves the potencies to realize them in the higher degree? We possess a modicum of life, a modicum of truth, and a modicum of love, but do we possess them in their entirety?

Life is not completely under our control. Each tick of the clock brings us closer to our end; "our hearts are but muffled drums beating a funeral march to the grave." "From hour to hour we ripe and ripe; from hour to hour we rot and rot." Even the very food we eat, while nourishing us, gradually corrodes and wears away the machinery of our body.

And while truth is a condition of our nature, it is almost like a phantom, for the more we study the less we know, or rather the less we think we know. Profound study opens up new vistas of learning, worlds quite beyond our

232

own, worlds of grace, each with laws of their own. How often too, a search after truth corrects the prejudices of youth; how often earnest seekers after the Logos have come to mock and remained to pray. Great minds have confessed that after a life dedicated to the quest for truth, they felt that they were merely standing on its shores, whilst its great expanse stretched out infinitely before them. Thomas Aquinas, the greatest mind of Christian times, declared at the end of his life that all he had written was a straw compared to a vision which Divine Truth had accorded him.

Finally, love in its perfected state is not found in this world. Broken hearts, ruined homes, divorce courts, all are eloquent proofs that man has not found true and lasting love. Love seems to be rich in its promise; and yet, through some mysterious ordering of things, it reaches a point of satiety, and when disorder sets in, it reaches the point of hate. Regardless of how happy human love is, a day of separation must come for those who love, and nothing is perfect that ends.

Though we are human beings, though we possess three fundamental inclinations, which are the very main springs of our being, yet we do not find these inclinations realized on this earth. Life is mingled with death; Truth is mixed with error; and Love is found with hate. Our life then is not in creatures; our truth is not in the spoken word; our love is not in what we see. Life cannot exist with death; truth cannot exist with error; and love cannot exist with hate.

But where find the source of these three realities? Where find Perfect Life, Perfect Truth and Perfect Love? Let us make the answer clear by an example. Suppose I was in search of the source of light that is in this room. I cannot find the source of light as long as I seek it in shadows, i. e., in a mixture of light and darkness. The source of light for that reason cannot be found in a corner, or under a chair or under a desk, for there light is mingled with darkness. Where find the source of light? I must go out to something which is pure light, viz., the sun. So too, if I am to find the source of the life and the truth and the love that is in this world, I must go out to a Life that is not mingled with its shadow death, out to a Truth which is not mingled with its shadow error, out to a Love which is not mingled with its shadow hate. I must go out to that which is Pure Life, Pure Truth and Pure Love—which is God.

"There is a quest that calls me
  In nights when I am alone,
The need to ride where the ways divide
  The Known from the Unknown.
I mount what thought is near me
  And soon I reach the place,
The tenuous rim where the Seen grows dim,
  And the sightless hides its face.
I have ridden the wind,
I have ridden the sea,
I have ridden the moon and stars,

I have set my feet in the stirrup seat
Of a comet coursing Mars.
And everywhere
Thro' the earth and air
My thought speeds, lightning-shod,
It comes to a place where checking pace
It cries 'Beyond lies God.' " [4]

And if we would sound the depths of God
Who is Life, Truth and Love, we need but go
into our own heart and our own experience.
The best of human things are but the dim, far-
off echo, the feeblest reflection, the fraction of
that which in God is perfect. If the possession
of life thrills and exalts us; if the conquest
or discovery of a new truth lifts us up to heights
of intellectual joy; if the human heart in its
noblest reaches and purest affections has the
power to cast us into an ecstasy of delight, then
what must be the great Heart of Hearts! If a
human heart can increase the joy of living then
what must be the great Heart of God! *If the
Spark is so bright, oh, what must be the Flame!*

[4] Cale Young Rice.   (9)